What readers say about

For Love and Money

"It's the first really honest account I've seen on how to deal with the sticky and embarrassing issues of wealth, which nobody else wants to talk about. It's a godsend."

> —Marjorie Kelly, Editor and Publisher, *Business Ethics*

"Roy Williams' book is a valuable resource for all families in business together. He points out, better than anyone in the field today, the importance of family teamwork and how to build a family team. This book will be added to our recommended reading list at the Owner Managed Business Institute."

> —Dr. John A. Davis, President, Owner Managed Business Inst., Santa Barbara, California

"Contains much practical wisdom for healing past difficulties, preventing future ones, and forging closer family bonds. Important learning for all family members."

> —Jordan Paul, psychologist, Director, Center for Community Partnering, Aspen Colorado, author of *Do I Have To Give Up Me To Be Loved By You?*

"Roy Williams supplies wise and workable advice on how to achieve one of the great tasks of life's Second Half—leaving a legacy that survives into the next generation."

> —Bob Buford, author of *Half Time* and *Changing Your Game Plan from Success to Significance;* Chairman, Buford Television, Inc.

For Love
& Money

A Comprehensive Guide
to the Successful Generational
Transfer of Wealth

Roy O. Williams

MONTEREY PACIFIC PUBLISHING, SAN FRANCISCO

Monterey Pacific Publishing

San Francisco

Library of Congress Catalog Card Number: 96-77608

ISBN 1-880710-01-3

Dedication

I would like to dedicate this book to my wife, Diana; to our three sons, Scott, Eric and Dan; to their wives, Mary Ellen, Kim and Nawshi; and to their children, Kyle, Andrew, Carly, Quinn, Jordan, Eric Jr. and Kyra. They are the ones who taught me the most about being in balance—as a father, husband and businessman. Thank you for contributing so much to my life. I love you.

Acknowledgments

Eight years ago when I began writing *Preparing Your Family to Manage Wealth*, the predecessor to this book, I thought it would be easy to dictate my thoughts, organize them and compile the book from ideas and tools for helping clients and their families. Little did I know how much help I would need and how much I would receive. The same process has repeated itself in preparing the material for this edition.

First I want to thank all of our clients over the last thirty-two years. You and your families were the ones who trusted us and went along with what must have appeared at times to be strange ideas. Your homes and offices were the classrooms where we learned ways to work, play, laugh and love together. They were where we learned how to build trust and how to explore and share our ideas in a safe environment. Without all of you, this company would not exist and this book could never have been written.

My thanks go to Fernando Flores, Phillip Hallstein and all of those at Business Design Associates, for their insight and coaching on the art of listening and building trust; and to Julio Olalla and Rafael Echeverria, for helping us become better coaches. I'm grateful to Ed Stanley for his sage advice and the analogy of taking the training wheels off the kids' bikes at some age—whether five or sixty; to Dean Edward C. Halbach, Jr., of the Boalt Hall School of Law, University of California, Berkeley, for his wisdom, judgment, objectivity and friendship. Thanks also to Theo Wells and Nori Huddel, both of whom spent many hours helping me dictate by asking good questions and challenging the clarity of my thoughts.

I especially want to thank the friends and clients who went through the drafts of the book and gave me many suggestions on better ways to communicate the points I was trying to make. They are:

- ❤ Art and Sarah Ludwick, Rain Bird Manufacturing Co.
- ❤ Robert and Wendy Graham, Katalysis Foundation, San Tomo Foods
- ❤ Budge and Arlene Brown, Brown Enterprises

- ❤ Kelin Gersick, Professor, California School of Professional Psychology, and partner in the Owner Managed Business Institute
- ❤ John Levy, specialist in inherited wealth
- ❤ Jordan Paul, psychologist and author
- ❤ Ginger Taylor, Communication Design
- ❤ Gordon Snyder, Communication Design
- ❤ Mary Villa, Client Services Manager
- ❤ Pat Mancebo, my able assistant
- ❤ John O'Neil, President, California School of Professional Psychology (retired)
- ❤ John Brady, President, Growth Technologies, Inc.
- ❤ Jim Pigott, Pigott Enterprises
- ❤ Pete Coors, Coors Brewing Co.

A special thank you to Colin Ingram, my collaborator, and the one person without whom this book would not have been written. Thank you, Colin, for your energy and sage advice.

And to everyone else who helped me: Thank you all.

Contents

Author's Comments

This book is based on my thirty-plus years experience in dealing with families of wealth. Over this time I have seen many changes in the nature of families; there are now increasing numbers of single parents, adults without children and families where females have assumed the leadership role.

But regardless of these changes, the basics remain the same. For example, no matter who is running the business or the family assets, and how they are related, trust and effective communication are still necessary fundamentals for success.

Where there are no children in a family, someone must still be educated and trained in the management of family assets if the family is to continue to prosper. So the tools I describe for educating family heirs are also valid for any other inexperienced persons who will someday be involved in running the family business and/or managing family investments. Similarly, the techniques presented for helping a family to become a working team are also valid for any group that needs to learn how to work together effectively.

Although I frequently refer to entrepreneurs and to family-owned and family-managed businesses, almost all of the information in this book also applies to employed individuals and their families who have inherited or built up assets through means other than an active family business. Management of substantial family assets is similar in many ways to the management of a business. It requires skills in dealing with people, delegating authority and achieving a high level of knowledge and expertise. It also involves considerable time. In effect, *the management of family wealth is, itself, a family business. So wherever I have referred to the family business, I specifically intend for the information to apply to the management of family wealth as well.*

In writing this book it has been convenient to frequently refer to the financial head of the family as male, to the spouse as female and to the family as a traditional one with a husband, wife and children. Yet I would like the reader to understand that the information presented is meant to apply equally to both genders and to a wide variety of family situations.

A point of usage in this book are the terms "children" and "kids." In many cases, the beings that parents give birth to and raise are still referred to as children even after they are fully grown. At age 89, my mother still calls me one of her children. It's true that the English language has a shortage in this regard—we simply don't have distinctive terms for our grown-up offspring. But what are the implications of calling them kids and children? Is this a box we put them in so that they never really grow up in our minds, and we behave accordingly?

Two of our clients are twin brothers, aged 65, who have three adult sons between them. The three sons, who are all in their mid-thirties, work in the family business and have always been called "the boys." Even the receptionist referred to them as "the boys." Just changing this pattern and calling them by their names changed the image of "the boys" in the office almost immediately and enhanced their credibility and performance. So when we as parents and grandparents refer to our adult offspring as "children," we should take care that we are not creating an unintended image in the minds of ourselves or others.

In this book I have tried to be sensitive to this problem. Nevertheless, the nature of the language requires that the term be used in some cases. So I ask your indulgence when I refer to grown-up offspring as "children," and that you will accept this usage with good grace.

The examples used throughout this book for amounts of income, investment, recreation, etc., vary widely. Where these amounts seem either excessive or insignificant in relation to your own situation, please understand that the information presented is applicable to a wide range of assets. In those instances where the ideas and techniques I present are limited to certain levels of assets or income, I specifically mention this. Especially, where substantial wealth is mentioned, readers should not be dissuaded because they are not (yet) multi-millionaires.

With the exception of a few instances where I have stated otherwise, the names of my clients mentioned in this book, their types of businesses and their locations have been changed in order to maintain confidentiality. Some of the circumstances and events I have described have been altered or simplified to clarify the point I want to make. Otherwise, the many persons I have portrayed in this book are based on real families in real situations.

And a final, very important point. From cookbooks, a reader can try new recipes and reasonably anticipate preparing some satisfying meals without the aid of a chef. Books on legal advice and flying lessons, in contrast, are quick to insist that they are not substitutes for sound professional assistance. This book falls into the latter category.

It has taken us at The Williams Group many years to understand all of the elements that are needed for the successful, generational transfer of wealth, and many more years to refine the techniques that have flowed from this understanding. One of the things we have learned is that each family is unique—one size doesn't fit all. So while this book will provide you with many insights and, hopefully, uplift your own vision of what is possible, it is not meant to be, nor can it be, a substitute for the personal coaching process.

Introduction

Most families with substantial businesses or other assets have estate planners. These planners are very competent in their field, yet most of these plans fail. In fact, research indicates 70% of family businesses do not survive the change from founder to the second generation, and close to 90% do not make it to the third generation.[1] The professional advisers retained by these familes don't know why this happens.

As we have worked with families in many countries of the world over the past thirty years, we have gained some clues. Here are a few quotes, related to this problem, from the parents of these families:

"My son isn't interested in going into the business—he hates the business and blames me for having made money with it."

"The kids just don't have the ability. I'm afraid they'll run the business into the ground."

"My children just want a free ride—forget about earning anything!"

"Somewhere along the way—I don't know exactly when—we just lost them. Now we just pretend we're a family."

And here are some quotes from the young or grown-up children of these families:

"If you have money you don't have to be honest or courteous or kind."

"I am ashamed of my family's wealth. I buy my clothes at thrift stores to make sure I don't look rich."

"All the things I know came from my nanny. I don't really know my parents at all.""My father only loves with money. He sends presents but he never shows up."

"I can never live up to Mom and Dad's expectations. I don't have any confidence at all."

"I hate my father for weighing me down with financial burdens I didn't want."

"There's no planning. We can't discuss our parents' death at all, or what happens after that."

"It's unfair. My brother is getting all the perks and my sister and I get nothing. But it's Mom's and Dad's money—how can we say anything?"

"Ever since Mom and Dad died, my brothers and I have been constantly fighting over money. We don't trust each other."

I could go on for pages with comments reflecting poor self-image, resentment, embarrassment, abandonment, frustration and need for love among the members of these families. What has caused such family discord and skewed values?

I recently spent some time with a father who kept telling me how many excellent deals he had recently made. From the tone of the conversation, I felt that this man had lost sight of what was really important, so I asked him a series of blunt questions. I asked him how much time he spent with his teenaged children. Did he ever spend time with them just simply listening? Was he satisfied with the role model he had created for them? Was he more concerned with his children acquiring values based on integrity or on values centered around making money? And lastly, if his family was important to him, could he justify the amount of time he spent away from them? His answers reflected the fact that this entrepreneur had done nothing to prepare his children to live wisely. For him, the acquisition of wealth has been accomplished but at a tremendous cost.

The number of families with potential problems of this kind is increasing. What kind of adults will spring from these families, and will they have the values, judgment and maturity to use the family assets wisely? Stories abound of inheritors who have dissipated the family assets and wasted their lives in the process.

In family after family we have worked with, we have witnessed children growing up with skewed values, communication within the family nonexistent, fathers or mothers estranged from their grown-up children and family members harboring resentment that twists and shapes their lives.

Few books or courses of instruction have been available for parents who want to raise mature, balanced children who are able to receive and responsibly use money they have inherited. This issue badly needs to be addressed. In our practice we see heirs battling over succession issues to the point where they waste millions upon millions of dollars in legal fees. We've watched families tear themselves apart over perceived unfairness in their inheritance. And we've seen vital, wealth-producing businesses, built up over a lifetime of effort, destroyed out of ignorance and lack of preparation.

The old ways of transferring assets to children and grandchildren, ways which rely solely on legal and tax tools, simply aren't working. We have to begin addressing a new paradigm of assets transfer—a whole new way of looking at this challenge is necessary.

This book introduces you to this new paradigm. We call it the Integrated Wealth Transfer Process™, a process we have been refining for many years. This book describes family meetings where an open atmosphere has been carefuly cultivated in order to speak freely about sensitive topics—money, succession, the family mission and the management of family assets. It shows how concensus is reached by changing performance standards for family members from unspoken and unclear standards to observable and measurable ones.

The information provided fills the gap for the generational transfer of wealth and knowledge. It tells you the basics on how to give your children—when they are young and when they have become adults—the knowledge and experience to use family assets effectively. The processes we describe in this book are not just theories—they are based on our actual experiences working with families for more than three decades. These processes are not quick fixes; ingrained family attitudes take time to change. But as you invest your time, energy and heart into them, they will yield many benefits. Your spouse and your grown-up children will be prepared to inherit your legacy and use it wisely. You will be giving your heirs the tools—the same tools you have used so effectively—which will enable them to develop their own skills that will last for generations. With these processes, you will empower your family to take control of succession; you will help them to deal confidently with authority figures; and your family will become a real working team, where decisions are based on sound information, trust and mutual respect.

A successful transfer of wealth to your succeeding generations means more than money. It means raising children who are strong enough to test and confirm your values in their own life experiences, and who will become competent, self-confident, generous and loving persons in their own right. And finally, the successful transfer of your values, as well as your wealth, means that the very best part of you will survive to benefit the lives of all your succeeding generations. You could not leave a greater legacy.

The purpose of ths book is to describe the Integrated Wealth Transfer Process™ and to give you a sampling of the challenges and the many rewards it bestows. But before your family members can learn to effectively manage family assets together, you will be involved with several processes that you haven't used before. And your ingenuity, your insight, your empathy and your tolerance will be tested again and again.

Like most of us, you will be a beginner at creating an effective family team, and beginners can become impatient, frustrated and exasperated with the pace of their progress. I personally received a meaningful lesson on beginning that I want to share with you, and I hope it helps you as much as it helped me.

As part of an exercise for company managers, each of us in the group was given three silk scarves and asked to juggle them. Of course, we were not particularly interested in scarf juggling but we were asked to go along with it. After about five minutes of dropping the scarves on the floor and picking them up, I decided it was a pointless exercise—a waste of time, so I stopped. My instructor asked me if I felt as exasperated as I looked. I told him, yes, that I didn't see the point of my standing there, throwing scarves into the air and picking them up again.

He then asked me if I was a master juggler or even a minimally competent juggler, to which I responded, "no." "In view of that," he said, "shouldn't you expect lots of scarves to be on the floor?" And he suggested that perhaps the cause of my frustration was that I was applying unreasonable standards to myself in assuming I would be at least minimally competent immediately.

The lesson, of course, was that I was not allowing myself to be a beginner, and that if I did so I would be less frustrated, I would learn more quickly and I would be a happier person. Now, each time I approach something new, I recall the silk scarves on the floor and I remember that I am a beginner. As you begin this new and exciting process of learning how to build a family team, I ask you to do the same.

1   Gal, Steven S., Director, USC Family Business Program, USC Business, Spring, 1995

Beckhard, Richard, and Dyer, W. Gibb, Jr., "Managing Continuity in Family Owned Business," *Organizational Dynamics*, Summer, 1983, pp. 5-12

Kets de Vries, Manfred F. R., "The Dynamics of Family Controlled Firms: the Good and the Bad," *Organizational Dynamics*, Winter, 1993, pp. 59-71

1 The Integrated Wealth Transfer Process™

Long Term Thinking

Even as we pursue our short-term interests, most of us still have a longing in the back of our minds for continuity, for a bridge to the future. I'm reminded of a charming story from Japan, about a man who walked along a rural road to and from his workplace. Each day, during his walk, he noticed a farmer treading on a water wheel in order to flood a rice paddy. But nothing was ever planted there. This went on year after year for twenty years until, when they were both old, the first man finally asked the farmer, "I've watched you doing this year after year, without planting. Why are you doing this?" And the farmer replied, "I'm preparing this field for my grandson."

In the United States there is now a tremendous lack of long term thinking. We read about it everywhere—in business, where the quarterly report is the most important thing in the world; in politics, where the future extends only to the next election; and even in sports, where the current season's standing outweighs the need for long-term team improvement.

This tendency to look at just the short term is also present in our grown-up children. If their parents are 50-60 years old, and we assume a normal life expectancy of 75-80 years, why, they ask, do they need to start worrying about their inheritance now? Aren't you, their parent, going to be around for another 20 years or so? Your sons and daughters have to be shown why it is important to prepare, and they need to understand that it takes time—preparation to use an inheritance wisely isn't something that will happen overnight.

Many Americans don't plan adequately for the future. When

we do, it's usually limited to our own lifetime. But if you have built up wealth that produces social benefits, or a business that provides good jobs for people, wouldn't it be a shame for all of that to disintegrate when it could continue to thrive and be a benefit to your heirs and to the world for generations?

At The Williams Group we take the long view. All of our work with families over the years has demonstrated that family assets can be a powerful tool for good; that they can be used to bring the family closer together now, to enhance the lives of our children and grandchildren in the future, and to help build a better world.

Like most parents, you've worked hard in the past to build a successful business or grow other assets. But your children were not active participants in doing that. Because they have been unable to share your experiences, there is a missing link between your own past and your children's future. There is a way to bridge this gap, and it is through your own personal values. We like to call this necessary link "bridge building," where your values, your experiences and your creations can become bridges that span the gaps between family members, between generations and between the family and the world.

Before we continue, I'd like to share something with you which I hold in high esteem. Written in 1898, it's called:

The Bridge Builder

An old man, going a lone highway,
Came at the evening, cold and gray,
To a chasm, vast and deep and wide,
Through which was flowing a sullen tide.
The old man crossed in the twilight dim—
That sullen stream had no fears for him;
But he turned when he reached the other side,
And built a bridge to span the tide.
"Old man," said a fellow pilgrim near,
"You are wasting strength in building here.
Your journey will end with the ending day;
You never again must pass this way.
You have crossed the chasm, deep and wide,
Why build you the bridge at the eventide?"

The builder lifted his old gray head.
"Good friend, in the path I have come," he said,
"There followeth after me today
A youth whose feet must pass this way.
This chasm that has been naught to me
To that fair-haired youth may a pitfall be.
He, too, must cross in the twilight dim;
Good friend, I am building the bridge for him."

Willamena Allen Dromgoole

The Three-Faceted Pyramid

Families with substantial assets almost always hire tax and legal experts to design and implement estate plans that will protect the family's assets after Mom and Dad are gone. Yet, as I mentioned in the Introduction, most estate plans fail—that is, most of the family assets don't even make it through the next generation. Why is this, given the fact that the hired advisers are experts in their field?

In recent years, our own conclusions at The Williams Group have been confirmed by independent research.[1] In general, here is what this research has shown. The successful, generational transfer of assets is dependent upon:

1) The degree of trust, openness, cooperation and mutual respect among family members.

2) The number of years the heir(s) worked full-time in the family business or managed family assets, and how well prepared the heirs felt at the time of succession.

3) The preparation of a formal succession plan, including a plan to train successors, and an effective working relationship with professional advisors.

All of the above are important factors. Putting it in terms of numbers, inadequate estate planning was found to contribute 10% or less of the reason for the failure to transfer family assets. The overwhelming preponderance—85% of the cause—is overlooked. This 85% is caused by 1) lack of trust and communication among family members, 2) heirs who have not been prepared to deal with the family assets, and 3) lack of succession planning (or out of date planning). In order to bring about the successful transfer of assets, each of these areas must be addressed.

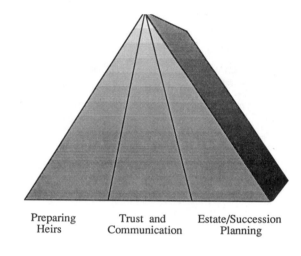

Preparing Heirs	Trust and Communication	Estate/Succession Planning

Of course, the problems and challenges are different, in detail, with each family. Working closely with each family, we help create an individual family plan—a roadmap—for successful wealth transfer. We call these plans the Integrated Wealth Transfer Process™ and we illustrate this process by a three-faceted pyramid as shown here. We use the pyramid to symbolize solidity and permanence, and its triangular, or delta, shape is the symbol for change. So we are trying to convey two things here: that change is necessary and that these changes, once accomplished, will result in solid, permanent improvements.

The process begins at the bottom of the pyramid. When a family has reached the apex in all three areas, they will have a very high degree of assurance of the successful transfer of their family wealth. Perhaps of equal importance, they will have become—*by their own admission*—a closer family where everyone is pulling together as a team.

Trust and Communication

One of the ways we illustrate the need to improve trust and

communication is by asking Mom and Dad to list their concerns that have to do with the family in some way. The items they list are usually quite varied, such as Mom feeling that Dad is absent too much of the time; that Dad is worried that their children will run the business into the ground and by his belief that they don't know the value of money; both Mom and Dad are concerned about how to treat the children and spouses of divorced marriages; and so on.

We typically end up with a list of 10-15 concerns, and when these concerns are matched up with the three areas of our pyramid, Mom and Dad are surprised to see that they fall in the three areas approximately as follows:

- 65% — lack of trust and communication
- 25% — heirs not prepared to manage assets
- 10% or less — inadequate estate planning

With this awareness, we begin the process of developing trust and communication. A first step in this process is to help family members to recognize the components of trust, and how it is broken and repaired. Part of this is learning how to listen—how to listen with the "third ear." Another element is the creation of an open atmosphere where, during family meetings, concerns that formerly remained hidden and were taboo subjects—topics such as discussion of the family's net worth, of succession plans or the lack of them—these kinds of topics can now be talked about openly. In fact, this atmosphere invites the broader discussion of, for example, what is the purpose of money? What is the purpose of having family wealth?

We show, through our process, how each family member has different perceptions of a given family concern, and why each person's view is worthy of being heard. Through the dynamic interaction procedures we employ, even formerly hostile family members are led to the point of making positive family contributions.

An exciting aspect of beginning the trust and communication learning process is that progress can usually be seen and felt at the outset. Longstanding family problems still require time to work out, of course, but there is a feeling that a significant start has been made.

Another aspect of beginning the trust and communication process is that family members become more informed. An increasingly informed family will begin to develop greater mutual trust. This is one of the most rewarding things that can happen to your family, and its benefits will reach into every aspect of your lives.

We'll go more deeply into the process of improving trust and communication in the chapters that follow.

Preparing Your Heirs

George Huntington Hartford II, heir to the A & P fortune, typifies the heir who was unprepared to receive wealth. Hunt, as he was known to his friends, was so isolated from the family business that he was in total ignorance of it when he inherited a ninety million dollar fortune. He hadn't been allowed to participate in financial affairs and had been given no instruction at all in money management. Wanting to make good use of his inheritance but not knowing how to go about it, Hunt indulged his one great interest— fine arts—by first investing in a California artists' colony which turned out to be a failure. His second major investment was an art magazine which soon folded. His third investment was an art museum in New York City which also failed. Even with many advisers around him, Hunt was bewildered. He couldn't distinguish the competent advisers from the incompetent ones, nor was he able to properly evaluate their advice. He spent thirty million dollars to develop an island resort in the Bahamas, but, shortsightedly, sold his interest before it became profitable. Hunt also spent huge sums on high living and drugs, which badly damaged his health.

Year after year, Hunt's fortune dwindled, the result of bad decisions, bad money management and imprudent habits. Today, only a fraction of the inheritance remains, and George Huntington Hartford II, living in isolation and poor health, looks back on a fortune for which he was unprepared and which proved to be his undoing.

While the amount of Hunt Hartford's inheritance was uncommonly large, his story is not at all uncommon. Though you, yourself, have probably built up your own business and wealth, your sons, daughters and other beneficiaries will have to deal with money coming to them which they didn't earn. The responsibilities that accompany wealth are part of their heritage; they didn't have a choice.

For all the sharp, tough, creative thought that Dad or Mom puts into their business, they almost never approach the continuity of their business or their grown-up children's ability to oversee the family assets with the same focus and determination. Is this the nature of things? Are your sons and daughters so different from you that they simply cannot acquire the skills that you now have? Of course, each family is different, but based on more than thirty years of experience helping families put their affairs together, we can say with confidence that lack of preparation is the common denominator that causes so many problems, and that you *can* prepare your children to responsibly inherit your wealth as well as your values.

Of course, passing on your wealth is much more than giving your grown-up children the ability to mind the store. What values will be passed on to them? Will money be more important to them than mutual consideration and respect? If so, there is a good chance your grown-up children will initiate lawsuits against each other, as happens frequently with inheritees. Do your grown-up children think that money is simply something to spend and have a good time with, or do they understand that the possession of wealth confers upon them the responsibility to also use it for the good of others? Will your sons and daughters think of the family assets simply as something that provides them with income, or will they be involved in their maintenance and further development?

Why bother teaching values to your children? Won't they learn them from their own experiences? The answer is an unequivocal "No!" The essence of what we call *civilization* is based upon passing knowledge and skills from generation to generation. If each generation of children had to reinvent the wheel, we'd still have solid stone wheels, or perhaps no wheels at all.

And what about the contractor approach to teaching your children values? That is, hiring someone else to do it for you? The problem with that is that it doesn't work. Your children do absorb values, but they're someone else's values—not yours!

In fact, the greatest legacy you can leave your children are your own personal values—your beliefs about honesty and consideration, straight-shooting, giving a dollar's work for a dollar earned, to name a few. Your own values have been tested throughout a lifetime of learning, making mistakes and picking yourself up to try again. These values have real worth, and many times in this book I'll be bringing up the subject of your values and how they affect your family.

Your personal values aren't the only ones we'll be looking at. By comparing your values with those of your spouse and your children, you'll discover shared family values. These family values can be used to form a family consensus and family priorities, which then lead to family actions. It's by performing family actions and working together as a team that your children will begin the long but fruitful path to becoming prepared to inherit wealth.

Estate and Succession Planning

In traditional estate planning, tax laws are understood and provided for, and distribution of the estate's assets are determined and documented. Yet this may leave large gaps that need to be filled. For example, if there is a family business, do the goals of the estate plan agree with the goals for the family business? Is there a timetable for Dad to gradually and methodically give up control of the business, or will succession be a crisis when Dad is forced to relinquish control through incapacity or death? What will be the affect on heirs of putting assets in a trust? Who will manage family investments, supervise family foundations or work with money managers and other professional advisers to fulfill the estate plan?

To begin to answer these types of questions, we need to include the element of succession planning to traditional estate planning. Estate planning, for many families, determines how *non-business* family assets will be used; succession planning determines how the family business will be controlled and guided. In both of these categories, we then address the issues of Mission, Structure and Role.

<u>Estate Planning</u> and <u>Succession Planning</u>

Mission

Structure

Role

Mission statements enable families to clarify the purpose of family assets and of the family business. One of the questions I posed in the above paragraph was: Do the goals of the estate plan agree with the goals for the family business? For example, can the needs of heirs and/or philanthropy be met without harming business operations? Or does the plan for rapid growth of the business preclude (at least, for a set period of time) distribution of estate assets or business dividends? If there are potential conflicts between the needs of the business and the needs of heirs, do the plans provide a systematic way of prioritizing needs?

Family missions are often unspoken and unknown or assumed—most of the estate planning missions we see are unspoken but are assumed to be for wealth preservation and tax reduction. The process of developing clear and unambiguous, written mission statements is an important part of estate and succession planning.

Structure is the more familiar part of estate and succession planning. This is the nuts and bolts of the plans. Wills, trusts, buy-sell agreements, family limited partnerships, foundations and gift programs are examples of components of Structure.

We've all seen structures that don't work—wills that are out of date; buy-sell agreements that conflict with the wills; documents that give heirs wealth based on reaching some arbitrary age, even though the heirs may not be responsible or accountable at that point; and documents that place one sibling in a position of authority over the others, creating a lifetime of conflict and bitterness.

An example that comes to mind is of a father who made his oldest daughter executor and trustee of his estate. This placed the daughter in a very difficult position when it came to granting requests for funds from her siblings and their spouses. The pressure on her became unbearable. One brother sued her, and they both wanted other family members to take sides. He lost, but the legal fees were in excess of $300,000. This prolonged fight cost the daughter her marriage, her health and ended her close family relationships.

This leads us to the third aspect of planning, which is Role. In our estate plan, who do we select as executor, trustee? Who handles the nonbusiness assets? Who selects the new money managers as they are needed? What role will Mom and Dad, Step-Mom or Step-

Dad play in the estate? What role will your lawyers play? Your CPA?

In your succession plan, who will own and who will control the family business in the future? Do the estate and succession plans take into account the difference between ownership, control and benefits from the family business or other enterprises? For example, if three heirs will own equal parts of the family business and only one of them is running it, with the attendant income and perks of management, will the other heirs resent this and turn to litigation to solve their dispute...especially if the business is unable to pay them dividends? Conversely, if the estate plan calls for *equal* treatment of the heirs, and they do not have equal responsibilities, abilities or desire for involvement with the business, is *equal* treatment *fair* treatment? And is *equal* treatment the most effective means of protecting and growing the family assets?

After succession, will key employees stay with the business or will they leave because they don't have confidence in the abilities or the intentions of the heirs? Has the succession plan taken this possibility into account and included the key employees in the planning process?

Putting It All Together

In this opening chapter my purpose has been to give you a brief overview of the elements that, together, form the Integrated Wealth Transfer Process.™ At this point there are two things that I'd like to emphasize: the first focuses on the word *integrated*. Effective estate and succession planning can't be done without concurrently preparing heirs to implement it, and the heirs will not be able to form an effective, working family team unless they have also learned how to communicate with each other openly and clearly. All three of the basic elements are necessary and closely interrelated: 1) trust and communication, 2) preparing heirs, and 3) estate and succession planning.

My second point concerns timing. Are the things we are doing now preparing the field for our children and grandchildren to manage family assets well? Will our future generations be able to manage family assets skillfully, to further themselves, to further the goals of the family and to be a positive influence upon the world? If so, we need to begin thinking and planning for the long term—and we need to begin now.

The Integrated Wealth Transfer Process™ is the most effective system we know of to help families reach their goals. Now we are ready to look more closely at some of the exciting and powerful tools of building trust and communication—tools that really work and that will make a profound difference in your family.

1   Michael H. Morris, Roy O. Williams and Deon Nel, "Factors Influencing Family Business Succession," The Williams Group Technical Report 1995-1.

Richard L. Osborne, "Second-Generation Entrepreneurs: Passing the Baton in the Privately-Held Company," 1991

See Wendy Handler, "Succession in Family Firms: a Mutual Role Adjustment Between Entrepreneur and next-Generation Family Members," and Elaine Kepner, "The Family and the Firm: a Co-Evolutionary Perspective," *Organizational Dynamics*, Summer 1983, pp. 57-70.

Howard H. Stevenson and William A. Sahlman, "How Small Companies Should Handle Advisers," *Harvard Business Review*, Vol. 88, No. 2 (March-April 1988), pp. 28-34.

Barnes and Hershon, "Transferring Power in the Family Business."

2 Trust and Communication

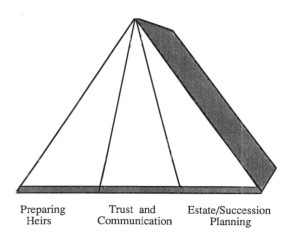

Preparing   Trust and   Estate/Succession
Heirs   Communication   Planning

We walked in and looked around before the meeting began. Seated in the room were Jim and Susan Weygand, Jim's son and daughter by a former marriage (both in their late 30's), and Susan's two sons, also by a former marriage (a little younger). The tentative subjects on the agenda were some portfolio decisions for the family investments.

This was not our first meeting with the Weygands, and we had all worked hard together to create a safe atmosphere for family communication. The ground rules we had established helped. These rules are: 1) Seek first to understand, then to be understood, 2) Anyone can raise any point or ask any questions without repercussions, 3) Only problems can be attacked, not individuals, and 4) If anyone is uncomfortable introducing a subject, then one of the members of The Williams Group, acting as family coach, will do it for him.

When the portfolio matters were concluded, Jim's daughter,

Lucie, said, "There's something that Dad's been avoiding that really bugs us. Last year Dad told us he was going to change lawyers and get one that we could all work with, but he never did. I've asked him three times but nothing ever happens." Then Susan's older son, Wade, added, "Dad's lawyer has the same answer for everything we suggest— 'I don't think that would be wise.' No matter what the subject is, it's always the same, 'I don't think that would be wise.' He treats us like school children. We just can't deal with that man."

Jim turned to me and grinned. He was proud of the way his and Susan's grown-up children were beginning to assert themselves. But Jim wasn't going to give up easily, and he said, "He's a good lawyer, and he's worked for me for twelve years." Jim's kids were silent—in the past, Dad's statements of this kind meant the conversation was ended, and they didn't know what to say. This was an appropriate point for me to intervene.

"Jim, we have an unworkable situation here, and I don't think anyone wants to put it under the table. It's something that is important to your children. What do you think we should do about it? What are the possibilities?"

This did two things: it restarted the discussion, and it demonstrated to his children that there are ways of bringing up important issues in a nonthreatening way.

It wasn't that Jim was especially obstinate, it was just that, for a long time, he had kept his business cards close to his chest. The result was that no one else in the family knew what was happening. Here was an opportunity to break that pattern. Jim resisted at first, but then opened up. He explained about some difficult litigation that was in-progress. The importance of the litigation, he felt, prevented him from changing lawyers at this time. One of his sons responded with, "But we didn't know that," and Jim's wife, Susan, added: "I didn't know that either." The discussion became a bit heated because there were some repressed feelings being aired for the first time. But the atmosphere was changed from past family meetings. These family members were starting to communicate with each other—really communicate—for the first time since we'd met them.

From his side, Jim admitted that he was used to making business decisions on his own, and that it just hadn't occurred to him to share this problem with his family. After discussing the litigation, Susan and all four sons and daughters agreed that it would be wrong to change lawyers at this time. But they extracted a promise from their Dad that as soon as the litigation was behind them, he would address the issue of a new lawyer—with them.

Jim had played the gentleman all through the meeting but he wasn't used to being challenged by anyone. When the meeting was over, he came up to me and said, "Roy, you've put me through the mill. I'm not sure I want to do this again." But just then the entire family approached Jim, and his daughter, Lucie, said, "Dad, I guess I never knew until today that sometimes you really get bothered by problems too. I feel closer to you now than I have for a long time. Thanks for having this meeting." The she hugged him and gave him a big kiss.

I grinned at Jim and managed to keep quiet while we all savored the moment. A short while later, we scheduled the next meeting.

At a future family meeting, the subject of the lawyer came up again. This time, there was a sound basis for making a family decision. Based on the needs of the business and some good input from all parties, the family decided to begin an immediate search for a new lawyer. This was a win-win situation. Everyone got something they wanted, plus the whole family got something it needed—more effective communication. It was a real turning point for the Weygands because this was the first time they had ever pulled together for a common goal.

What are the ingredients for really effective communication? Over the years we have been very active in participating in and sponsoring research on effective communication. The results show that it has several components. Let's begin by looking at our perceptions.

Family members' perceptions of each other are often quite different, and these differing perceptions may hinder communication. One of our tasks as coaches is to make sure that family members are able to get their important messages into the open, clearly and honestly. I recall a meeting with Frank Russo and his 24-year-old son, Paul. Frank had divorced his wife several years earlier. During the meeting, Frank just blew up at his son. He said in a loud voice, "You go down to L.A. to see your Mother, right? About once every few months, right? How many times have you called *me* in the last year? None! Not a single, damned time, and you live less than 20 miles away!"

Paul was taken aback, but he recovered quickly and replied in kind, "You're always too busy, so I stopped calling. Besides, I didn't think you cared!"

There was a moment of quiet, and then I asked each of them to try to interpret what was really going on—what they had really meant under the harsh words. After an exercise of reflective listening, the hurt feelings were acknowledged and respected, along with the need to see each other more frequently.

As hurtful as this brief exchange was, Frank and Paul understood that beneath the accusations, father and son *did* care for each other; they just had to learn to express it in a better way. This exchange between them was a new beginning in being open and honest. Though much more communication between them was needed, it was a start toward acknowledging the real love they felt for each other.

Effective communication is an art. As Alfred Viera, a communications specialist of Business Design Associates puts it, "...the words that are spoken are never sufficient to provide all the meaning that a given speaker intends to convey."[1]

Some communication problems within families are due to different perceptions of roles. For example, in a business setting when a CEO father asks his accountant daughter to get him a cup of coffee at the office, he is not just making a simple request, he is also sending a signal about the terms of the relationship and its history. He assumes that he has the right to ask her and that she will obey. But what if she were to reply, "No, Dad, why don't you ask one of the other vice-presidents?" or "That's a job for your secretary." Then they would be arguing over the rules of their relationship. She would be calling upon the assumptions of a work relationship, while he assumes the family relationship is still in effect.

In family meetings there are exercises we use that demonstrate how perceptions of the same thing can differ through biases—cultural, gender and personal. As a simplified example, when North Americans are asked to describe what they see in the draw-

ing below, most say a house with a window, and an adult and two
children standing beside it. However, when people in rural Kenya

are shown the same drawing, they describe it as two children with
a woman on her way to market, carrying a package on her head,
walking by a tree that has been denuded by elephants and giraffes
(only women carry packages to market). As soon as this Kenyan
impression is mentioned to us, we can see the situation through
the eyes of the Kenyans. Similarly, if the Kenyans have been to a
city or town with rectangular buildings and windows, and we
explain our interpretation to them, they are also able to see it
through our eyes.

When we work with families we introduce a new understanding of communication which is very powerful. I'll see if I can summarize this briefly. For thousands of years, human beings have
used language in a certain way. Linguists call it *representationalism.*[2] What this means is that when we want to convey information to someone else, all we have to do is to speak clearly enough
and the recipient will understand the information exactly as we
have understood it. In this view, if our words are carefully chosen,
they are like a telephone wire that passes the signal from speaker
to listener without alteration.

This type of communication is sometimes called the accounting view of language. It assumes there is an objective truth out there just waiting to be explained to someone else. It also assumes that a listener is "right" only if he understands the message in exactly the same way as the speaker, and he is "wrong" if he understands any part of it differently. Thus begin the age-old battles of who is "right" and who is "wrong."

While this understanding of communication has served us fairly well in the past, it has also led to much miscommunication and trouble. In families, it enables one or more persons to claim ownership of the "truth," that there can only be one truth. This precludes any meaningful dialog.

But in recent years linguists have described a new understanding of communication—they call it the *generative view of language.*[3] In this view, all information, descriptions, events and stories are altered through our individual filters of culture, history, personal background and mood. We each create our own version of what is "right." In fact, through this view of communication, we are all "right."

Now there are circumstances where representationalism is necessary. If we are building a bridge, we all have to get the specs correct or the bridge will fail. But if we are interested in human needs, motivation, desires and goals, generative communication has practical benefits. It is future-oriented. Instead of emphasis being placed on who is right and who is wrong, this view of communication asks, "How will my understanding of this conversation and your understanding of it shape my future and your future?" "Will this conversation help us to generate common action?"

When we learn to communicate in this way, new vistas open up, new avenues are seen. So learning to be aware of our differing perceptions isn't just idle entertainment—it helps build compromise, mutual understanding and trust. When family members have had some experience in understanding the differing perceptions of others, the next time there is a family conflict they are better prepared. For example, on one occasion when a family member threatened another by mentioning the possibility of a lawsuit, before it got out of hand the others said to him, "Each of you has a point—but we don't need a lawsuit—let's see if we can reconcile this among ourselves."

In my own family we make use of the illustration that I showed on the previous page. When my sons and I occasionally get into a right/wrong discussion, one of them will say, "We know, Dad! You're from Kenya."

There is a close interrelationship between perceptions and trust. If basic trust exists between family members, then differing perceptions among them are solvable problems. If I say a color is blue and you say it is green, there are several ways we can find a common ground. We can agree to call it blue-green, or we can agree to find a color chart and abide by its nomenclature. Whatever way we choose, there are some underlying assumptions: that we both want a fair solution to our differences in perception; and we trust each other enough to know that neither of us will try to cheat or harm the other in order to gain a decision in our favor. Similarly, in family disagreements, if there is basic trust between family members, differences in perception can usually be discussed and an agreement can be reached. Lack of trust, on the other hand, is a much more serious and difficult problem.

Sincerity is a necessary ingredient of trust. If a family member consciously and deliberately wishes to be insincere and untrustworthy there's not much we can do about it. But this is very rarely the case, even if it seems like it initially. Here's an example (simplified) that occurred in Ben Abrams' family that begins with his daughter, Becky, addressing his son, Johnathan.

"Johnny, you haven't been doing your share of the work. I think you're untrustworthy, and whenever we talk about it you always try to weasel out of it. So I've gotten discouraged. I don't trust you anymore." Becky wasn't the only one who had voiced this; the other family members had said something similar.

One of the things we emphasize in family meetings is the need to listen—really listen. So I asked Johnathan, "Will you please repeat what Becky just said?" He repeated her words pretty accurately. Then I asked him: "Is there something else behind her words that she didn't say? What do you think is her ultimate intention, her goal in saying this to you?"

This is a very important point in our work with families. We devise frequent listening exercises to learn how to hear what someone's real intent is behind their words. In this particular case, there was a lot of guessing, but eventually Johnathan got to the nitty-gritty, and said: "She wants—they all want—to be able to trust me."

I continued: "But they don't trust you. Are you satisfied with that? If you could get away with it, would you be willing to live the rest of your life with people not trusting you?"

"No."

"Would you rather they be able to trust you?"

"Sure."

During the course of this meeting, Johnathan committed to working with us and the other family members. We handed out some homework assignments to each member of the family which were designed to reinforce Johnathan's new behavior pattern. They worked—not perfectly at first—but over the next year he was a changed young man, and there was a noticeable increase in the level of mutual trust in Ben's family.

Johnathan *was* basically sincere. He just needed to directly face the effect his behavior was having on others in order to bring out that sincerity.

Another necessary ingredient of trust is reliability. Unfortunately, it's not uncommon for this to be absent between parents and children even though they are unaware of it. For example, Dad, as entrepreneur, holds high ethical standards in business. His "word" means something among his associates—when he gives it, he keeps it, and they all know it and can depend on it. If Dad hadn't been keeping his promises in his business dealings, he would never have been successful the way he has become.

So it's strange to see Dad's reliability in family dealings fall short of his proclaimed standards. This most often happens in "little" things—that is, things that are little to Dad but not to the children. When Dad says he'll be home at 4:00 p.m. to watch his son's tennis match, will he make the same effort to be on time as he does for a business conference? Will Dad be late, or will he call home that day to say that some "important" business problem has come up and he won't be able to make it?

"Little" things; like when Dad says he'll stop and pick up the corsage for his daughter's dance, and then forgets all about it. (Somehow, he never forgets to bring his notes to a business conference.) Whether or not Dad keeps his word on promises to the family determines, for them, his level of reliability and the degree of trust with which he is viewed. He may have a reputation as a dependable, square-dealing businessman and still fail miserably at home.

Dad's own behavior, in relation to what he says, is also closely watched by the children, even if it is not expressed. When Dad preaches to his boys about never drinking and driving, and they see him come home intoxicated, their trust in him is diminished and, over time, it can impact on everything else he says. If Dad tells the boys to always show respect for their Mother and then he puts her down in the boys' presence, he, himself, loses their respect. After watching this kind of behavior, the children think, "What you do is so loud I can't hear what you say," and they simply stop listening.

It's important for Dad to follow through on family commitments and to live up to what he preaches to the children. Dad has no more justification for reneging on a deal with the family than he does with the business. Reliability is one of the necessary ingredients of family trust. Without trust, whether it is between husband and wife, parents and children, business partners or even between countries, communication can't be really effective.

Trust is a sacred gift one gives and receives, based upon merit, and it can also be taken back quickly. How do you gain trust and how do you decide when to give your trust? If a son or daughter makes a mistake with money and gets into debt, or irresponsibly gets into an auto accident, the parents will often withdraw their trust and start to feel that their child is not trustworthy in other areas as well.

But there are different areas of trust. If your children are grown, you might trust them to drive a car, go grocery shopping or do reasonably well at bike riding. But would you trust them as brain surgeons? Would you trust them to manage the family assets? It depends, doesn't it, on their competence in each area?

When we work with families, together we identify the areas in which they're concerned about trust. Then we look at the three roots of trust: sincerity, competence and reliability. From these, we can begin to see where we may be placing trust erroneously or where we may be witholding trust to our own and others' detriment.

Time and time again we see situations in families, where the lack of competence or reliability is well known, but parents still

continue to give their grown-up children and their spouses responsibilities they are unprepared for and cannot fulfill. The same
thing is true when parents know their son or daughter is insincere. They gloss it over because they are unwilling to acknowledge the problem, but they place responsibilities on him or her in
spite of it, simply hoping for the best.

The key to building trust is to understand the necessity for
sincerity, competence and reliability to *all* be present. If they do
not exist together, we are being unfair to ourselves and to others
when we expect a certain level of performance from them. By being aware of the absence of either sincerity, competence or reliability in our grown-up children, spouses, employees or others,
we can offer the kind of help that will enable them to accept greater
and greater challenges and to become trustworthy. And by so doing we will eliminate a lot of conflict.

It's important to understand that trust is not a static, permanent state, it is a temporary assessment that can change. We
shouldn't assume that someone can never be deserving of our trust.
While we begin by assessing a person's sincerity, competence and
reliability, and thus the level of our trust, we can then move to the
next step: what kind of coaching or other assistance do they need
to improve? Can we, in a constructive, nonthreatening way, communicate to them their need to improve? Can we do this in such a
way that they will want to improve? If I tell someone, "I don't
trust you to do this," and stop there, that's the end of the discussion. But if I say to that person: "I want to be able to trust you. For
me to be able to increase my trust in you, I need to see you improve in the area of reliability. I'm willing to help you do that if
you're willing to try."

The need for change has been couched in the form of a suggestion, not a command. The recipient doesn't feel attacked. That
leaves psychological space for a calm and rational response. Trust
among family members is a prerequisite not only for good communication but for learning to work as a team. With trust,
there is room to develop mutual understanding. Within the family, you start to learn about each other, what each person's skills
are, what each has to offer, and how to deal with an individual's
weak points. Maybe there is one individual the rest of the family
tends to discount all the time, and they focus on his weaknesses

rather than on his strengths. Maybe, when he has an idea, he doesn't think it through all the way. That doesn't mean his idea has no value, it just means that the family needs to ask him a lot more questions to see if the idea is really valid.

When the family looks carefully at the merits of an idea, regardless of who thought of the idea, that's good communication. When the family learns to make use of everyone's skills, allowing each person to contribute to the extent of their ability, that's real teamwork.

Family communication in general will be difficult and no one will know what the underlying problem is until the lack of trust is recognized and candidly discussed. There are ways to build trust which I discuss in Chapter 6, but rebuilding trust that has been lost requires a strong commitment by all family members.

Differing perceptions among family members are often prolonged because of taboo subjects. One of the aims of family communication is to eliminate as many subjects as possible from the list of unmentionables. Some of the subjects that are commonly taboo are: How much wealth does the family actually have? How will the family decide if the grown-up children are competent to handle wealth? How will the wealth be divided among the grown-up children? When is Dad going to retire and (if sons or daughters are going to become involved with the business) when will he give up control? What happens when Dad dies (or Mom, if she is the family entrepreneur)? What liabilities will the grown-up children incur when Mom and Dad are both dead? And how will the spouses of those children be treated without creating marital problems?

During family meetings, it's interesting to observe that a subject is no longer taboo once there is a safe atmosphere for candid give-and-take and the subject has been openly discussed. Division of wealth and control among siblings is often unmentionable, initially. In one case, a family's younger daughter was more qualified than the older son to take over the family business. It took great effort to get the subject on the table, but once it was brought up, all kinds of questions could be asked. The son asked, "Can I live with my sister being President even though I'm older and I've been the big brother all of my life? Is there any position in the company I can take with my sister as President? Should I just bail out of the business? If I bail, can I live with the fact that my sister will be making a large salary and I won't?"

These are the kinds of questions that must be asked. Sometimes, the answers won't be known for years. In the above case, the son might decide that he can't be in the same company while his sister is President. That's okay because it's honest. In that case, alternatives can be found which will allow the son to get out of the business but still receive some income from it that doesn't harm business operations. And if the son doesn't believe that his sister will run the company well enough to appreciate his share of the business assets over the long term, a buy-and-sell agreement can be arranged that is fair to all.

When Mom and Dad are older, and the grown-up children have become aware of the large tax liability they will incur when both parents are gone, what can they do? Can they approach Mom and Dad and say, "We need to talk about your deaths?" They're afraid Mom and Dad will think: "You greedy kids, trying to get our money." And Mom and Dad don't want to talk about dying because it's uncomfortable. So everyone avoids the subject and, if nothing is done to plan otherwise, the kids receive such a large tax bill that the business may have to be sold or liquidated—sometimes at a fraction of its worth.

Sometimes, Mom and Dad are afraid to discuss certain topics. They may refuse to acknowledge, for example, that one of their sons acts foolishly and is not competent enough to take on business responsibilities. When this is the case, they are so habituated to treating all the children equally while they were growing up that it's very hard for them to do what is *right*. The parents are afraid of hurting their grown-up childrens' feelings, afraid of making them angry and afraid of being accused of unfairness. Unless they are able to discuss the situation and work out a reasonable solution, they are setting the stage for lawsuits between the siblings, and continuing bitterness.

Sometimes, a lack of communication results in unintended, or opposite, messages being sent. In one case, a client of ours, Tom Wilbanks, gave his daughter, Lynn, $10,000 to invest any way she desired. She immediately put the money into CD's and kept it there. For years, Tom had been griping about the stock market, about the incompetent managers of mutual funds, and about the questionable ethics in commodities trading. On top of that, Tom complained about the instability of real estate investments. Lynn got the clear (though unintended) message from all of this: "Investments are dangerous—play it safe." She was terribly afraid of making a mistake and losing *her Dad's money*, even though he had said it was hers. Aside from his skeptical comments about investments, her father had never tried to teach her anything about investing. He just assumed that she would somehow have this ability.

There was another Tom—Tom Tandy—who has a 19-year-old boy named Rick. Rick told me, "I don't trust my Dad." I asked him why, and he said, "Because he lied to me." "Come on," I said, "what did he lie about?" Rick said, "He told me that when I turned sixteen he would buy me a new car if I passed the driver's test. After I passed the test, I reminded him about the car and he said we couldn't afford it now—I'd have to wait. That company of his is worth more than ten million dollars and he can't afford a car? I'll never trust him again!"

Rick was nineteen when I met him. By a combination of earning money from a part-time job and help from his father, Rick got his car a year later, but, secretly, he never forgave his father for going back on his word earlier.

The incident of a parent having a cash crunch is not uncommon—it happens in all businesses from time to time. But in this case, Tom never took the time to explain that to his son; he was always too busy with business problems. Rick, for his part, never communicated his resentment to his father, and, after three years, his distrust has solidified. Today, Tom senses that his son holds a grudge against him but he is still too busy to find out why.

Learning to listen with the "third ear" is one of the requirements for good communication. But how does someone go about listening with the third ear? We have found that careful listening to the moods, concerns and other expressions in a person's voice helps to identify what is really going on. From this, we can piece together the recurring problems that are causing the family to be disfunctional.

By listening for the feelings beneath the words we can better predict the actions someone may take (or lack of actions if the mood is one of resignation or despair). By sensitive listening, we can help anticipate and plan the actions that will be needed to resolve those concerns

In their book on family relationships, Drs. Jordan and Margaret Paul state it like this: "All of the many varieties of responses to a conflict come from only two basic motives or intentions: 1) the intent to learn—an openness to learning from the conflict, which leads to loving behavior, or 2) the intent to protect—defending against any potential pain that might come from the conflict, which leads to unloving behavior. Any response other than an openness to learning is a protection."[4]

In all of our family meetings, when there is a conflict, we make sure that we say, "Look, we don't know if what you're saying is real. Is this how you really feel, or do you want to say something else? Are you possibly speaking from some kind of fear...fear of offending someone, fear of looking foolish, or fear of facing something unpleasant?" All of these mask the person's true feelings and prevent effective communication.

Getting all of the family members informed is one of the goals of these discussions. Yet some dads deliberately try to keep other family members uninformed. A few years ago, a woman asked me to look into her finances. Her husband had recently died without having told her anything about the state of their affairs, and she literally didn't know if she had enough money to buy food. He had been a scheming old codger who had liquidated most of his assets except his business. He had a son who was involved in the business, but before the Father had died, he had sold the business out from under his son without telling him. The Mother had no idea any of this was happening. When we investigated her assets, it turned out she was quite wealthy. Communication had been her husband's lowest priority, even as he faced death.

Sometimes, both parents conspire to keep their children uninformed. It's like this with Phil and Jessie Kronner who live in Southern California. Their net worth is several million dollars. They don't discuss money with their children. When I asked them why, they said, "Because the kids (aged 20 and 23) aren't ready." Phil and Jessie are even reluctant to talk about money with each other. The problem is, they don't like to think of themselves as being wealthy—it embarrasses them.

Whatever the reason, their children are grown up now but they are still uninformed. Not only are the son and daughter ignorant about handling wealth—the subliminal message they receive from their parents is, "We don't trust you."

In family after family, what most children want is more communication, especially with a reticent Dad. When the children get to pick Dad's brain and find out what's really happening with the business and investments, it becomes very exciting. When all family members are informed, the whole family gets excited, especially when advisers are brought into the family meetings. We bring the banker, the lawyer and the accountant to the meeting, and we listen to them. Everyone hears how Dad deals with them. Sometimes Dad or Mom won't accept the advice of an adviser—for rational or irrational reasons. For example, Dad may say that he doesn't want to sign a will, but he is unwilling to give his reasons. After much prodding, his true feelings begin to surface and he admits that he has a feeling that if he signs a will, he will die because his sister died one day after she signed her will. That's okay because it is honest communication, from the heart. In this case, we were able to get Dad to create a living trust so he doesn't have to sign a will. But the important thing is that Dad has been open and honest, so everyone in the family knows what is going on.

One way to ease into uncomfortable or difficult subjects is to ask for a "conversation of possibilities." For example, in a family meeting a son might say to his father, "Dad, I'd like to have a conversation about estate planning and your successor, but I'm afraid it might offend you, and I don't want to intrude on your privacy. Could we just discuss the possibility of having that kind of conversation?"

This is just talking about possibilities, without committments. With a conversation about possibilities, it might give Dad some space to think about it, or Dad might give some legitimate reasons for why he is uncomfortable talking about succession right now. At least this clears the air and it lays the groundwork for more discussion later. A conversation of possibilities has another benefit. Often, some family members are quick thinkers and others are slower and more reflective. The more reflective ones can feel threatened by having to come to a rapid decision. But if everyone knows that only possibilities are being discussed—no actions at this time—than the pressure is off and a more effective and comfortable exchange can take place. This is how international diplomacy is effective; you begin just with possibilities and then you proceed (with some luck) to commitments, and then to actions.

I recall an especially good communications breakthrough in Cecile Coleman's family—she's the entrepreneur of the family. Cecile and her husband are socially responsible people, and they've accomplished much good with their money. They have two sons and three daughters. The social responsibility has rubbed off on the daughters but not—at least not yet—onto the sons. At one of our first meetings, the daughters wanted the family to stop investing in lumber companies operating in the Pacific Northwest as a protest against cutting down old-growth forests. The sons countered with, "Those people up there are nearly starving to death...they need the jobs more than they need to save the trees. Besides, you don't have all the facts."

The sons kept ridiculing the daughters in a heavy-handed way and the meeting got very emotional. The daughters cried, and complained that the sons always got their way, that Mom and Dad never listened to them. There were too many strong passions flying around to accomplish anything at that moment, and there was too little factual information. The daughters, though sincere, were not presenting their case in a way that the other family members could respect. We suggested that they compile an information file and document their causes, including the consequences of removing selected investments from the family portfolio.

So the daughters started gathering social and environmental data to back up their positions and, with help from Dad, the effects on their portfolio return from divesting. We also coached them on how to stick to the issues and avoid personality conflicts. At the next family meeting, the daughters presented their information to their brothers and to both parents. Their presentation was well received by all family members. The fact that the daughters were now presenting their views in a more credible manner helped to soften the social perceptions of the sons considerably. Eventually, a compromise was reached. The daughters chose the five most important investments to eliminate from the family's portfolio, and everyone accepted that.

This was the beginning of a more trusting relationship between all family members. It didn't happen overnight—it took about one year before they all began to really trust each other's opinions, but the end results were very satisfying. The daughters made comments such as, "I'm not fighting with my brothers anymore," or "Now I don't have to walk on eggs around Dad." All family members agreed that many positive changes had occurred.

We at The Williams Group are sometimes asked, "What's the difference between your work on trust and communication and family counseling? Why shouldn't my family just hire a psychologist or family counselor to learn to communicate better?" It's a good question. For a start, we don't practice psychotherapy, and we don't delve into subconscious motives or events from the past. Our firm has a clear focus: we address the problem that 85% of family businesses and other family assets do not remain in family hands past the third generation.

We work on these issues by building communicaton and trust within the family. But learning communication skills in the abstract is relatively ineffective. What is necessary is to tie these skills directly to the practical details of succession and estate planning, the preparation of heirs to use family wealth efficently and wisely, and so on.

We coach but do not analyze. Our job is not to reveal *why* family members have certain personality traits, but to enable families to use these individual traits for the common good of the family. We help families learn new ways of communicating, we encourage new conversations and we demonstrate the possibility of new actions for the future.

So it isn't our purpose to replace psychological counseling. What we are doing is helping to build mutual trust, which is the necessary first step that leads to the effective transfer of wealth and wisdom. The result of this more effective communication and increased mutual trust is an increasingly informed family, a family that is starting to pull together. This is one of the most rewarding things that can happen to your family, and its benefits will reach into every aspect of your lives.

And how about your particular family? In recent years we have surveyed some 750 families. By far and away, they rate the issue of trust and communication as the most important to them. And yet, many families remain in denial over this issue.

When we first speak with families the initial conversation often goes like this: "We have a wonderful family. Certainly we trust one another and we love each other. Those trust and communication problems you mention don't exist in our family."

When asked if anyone in the family is incompetent in the area of managing the family business or the family investments, the most common type of answer is, "Well, I wouldn't say incompetent...." But then if we ask, "Are you prepared to give them the family business or the family net worth to manage?" the response is, "Not right now." If we ask further, "Can you anticipate a time in the future when you'll feel comfortable placing them in charge?" they will typically say, "I'm not sure if ever."

All this is to say that in many families we tend to anesthetize ourselves to the reality of our relationships. In fact, it is our experience that essentially all families can benefit from enhanced trust and communication. It is an integral part of creating the basis for the successful transfer of wealth.

1   Viera, Alfred A., "Notes On Communication and Listening," Business Design Associates, Inc., Emeryville, California, July 9, 1991

2, 3   Fernando Flores, Business Design Associates, Emeryville, CA

4   Paul, Jordan and Margaret, *If you Really Loved Me,* Compcare Publishers, Minneapolis, MN, 1987

3 Family Meetings and the Family Coach

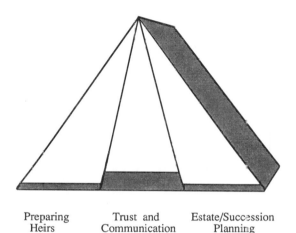

Preparing   Trust and   Estate/Succession
Heirs   Communication   Planning

With the information in the previous chapter on trust and communication, we have begun to make some progress in the Integrated Wealth Transfer process™. To further this progress we now join James Keel's family, as they are about to convene a family meeting. Sarah Keel, James' wife, has agreed to chair the meeting, her first as Chairman. The Keels' three grown-up children—two daughters and a son—are there (ages, 27, 25 and 24). Also present at this particular meeting are their lawyer and their accountant. And finally, a family coach, a person highly skilled in guiding these meetings, is attending.

Mom, who is chairing this meeting, calls it to order and distributes agendas to those who have not already seen them. Prior to this meeting, Mom has worked closely with the family coach (a highly trained staff member of The Williams Group) to develop today's agenda. The first agenda item is to agree on observable and measurable goals of what the family wants this meeting to accomplish by the end of the day. Having agreed to these goals, the next topic is how to proceed with forming a family partnership. Dad has worked with his advisers and our team to determine an appropriate partnership for this particular family. Dad now begins by explaining the purpose of the partnership and then asks the family's lawyer a series of questions. The lawyer answers the first question but then appears to waffle on the next one. Dad doesn't accept this, and further questions the lawyer on this topic. Mom, the daughters and the son listen closely; this is a side of their Dad they've never seen—how he deals with his advisers. The lawyer then promises to get the desired information to the family within the week, and Dad thanks him courteously for his input. Agreeing to plug in the missing information when the lawyer delivers it, the family members are still able to detail the necessary steps to establishing their partnership.

Mom then brings up the next topic on the agenda, which is to discuss who among the three grown-up children are now willing to definitely commit themselves to joining the family business. Dad dominates the conversation, but when he has finished, the coach faces Dad's grown-up children and says, "We'd like to hear what each of you think about your potential involvement with the business. Perhaps there is more you'd like to know about the business that will help you decide?" The coach doesn't ask this out of the blue; he has previously been interviewing the family members and helping them identify their concerns. Encouraged by this process, Katie, the oldest daughter, addresses Dad: "I don't know if I want to be involved. You've always been so secretive about the business that I have no idea what it's really like." The others also plead ignorance and add similar charges aimed at Dad. He cringes but grins. In spite of the criticism, he is very pleased with the progress they are making and that his son and daughters are now able to be forthright with him. Dad says, "Alright, we can fix that. On Thursday morning, 9:00 a.m. sharp, we're all going on a grand tour of the plant."

Will, the youngest of the siblings, is emboldened by Dad's positive reaction, and he says, "Dad, I'd like to do more than just tour the plant—I'd like to see the sales and profit figures." Dad cringes again, then replies, "Can we do the tour first? I'd like to handle one thing at a time." His children agree, feeling they have pushed Dad enough at this time, but they write notes to remind themselves to bring this up at the next family meeting.

Later in the day, Mom gives a summary of what has been accomplished by this meeting and what each participant is expected—and has agreed—to do within a given time frame. Mom then adjourns the meeting.

In addition to the specifics that have been discussed, the family members have been introduced to Dad's lawyer and his accountant. They've already met with the family coach but from the meeting they've had an opportunity to see how the coach operates with other family members. From this meeting, Mom has learned considerably more about the family business and, through her chairing the meeting, has gained a sense of sharing control of important family matters. The son and daughters have, for the first time, found a safe forum for speaking candidly to their parents about things that have been concerning them for a long time but which were previously taboo subjects. And for the first time in years, the members of the Keel family are beginning to really communicate with each other.

Of course, this brief description reveals only a tiny portion of everything that transpired during this family meeting, but it illustrates the nature of the proceedings and the kinds of things that can be accomplished.

The family meeting is one of the best ways we have found to create an atmosphere for effective communication within the family. These meetings are not for casual, daily decisions of the family, but for addressing important topics and dealing with the strong feelings they produce. Formalizing family meetings offers several advantages. First, the formality of the meeting says to sons and daughters that this is important—it isn't a discussion Mom and Dad have called in order to decide what color to paint their kitchen. Second, having an advance agenda encourages the participants to think seriously about the topics. Third, the presence of persons from outside the family augments the seriousness of the meeting's purpose.

While the agenda gets everyone thinking, the course of the meeting need not follow it inflexibly. For example, a family may meet to talk about a family partnership but as the discussion warms up, the subject of real interest turns out to be a divorce that happened five years ago, and the anger that the sons and daughters still feel about it.

Family meetings typically include all family members, including the spouses of grown-up children, and young children who are mature enough not to disrupt the proceedings. In preparation for the meeting, the coach has interviewed all family members who will attend. It is important for this to be done by an independent person in order to ascertain if problems exist that cannot easily be addressed by family members. At this time, the coach also introduces attendees to effective communications practices that help them to deal with difficult topics.

The coach attends all family meetings. Also attending, on an as-needed basis, are the key family advisors: the lawyer, accountant, money manager, and so on. Each one of these managers, or specialists, addresses the group, reporting on his or her activities on behalf of the family.

Even family members who are hostile usually attend family meetings. Even if they don't show up at first, once they learn where the action is they'll come if only to find out what's happening. Surprisingly, hostile family members often play a beneficial role. The one who is the perennial irritant, who asks antagonistic questions and seems to be deliberately obstructive, is actually making an important contribution. First, his or her presence teaches the family how to deal with the anger and frustration that are disruptive to the proceedings. Second, and more important, what this angry person is saying may really be significant. He or she isn't afraid to challenge the system or to point up personal errors. If the other family members can learn to listen to what is behind the anger, they'll often find that there is some basis for the comments.

After a hostile feeling has been expressed, we might say to that person, "You have just said something important, and we'd like to make sure everyone is listening to you" Then the coach might address the entire family and say, "We've heard how he feels, now how can we address this issue and how can we change the mood of what's just been said to make it more constructive?" When appropriate, the coach takes the group through a listening exercise which changes the whole complexion of the discussion.

Very often, the hostile feeling expressed is a result of never having really been listened to, and when the entire family learns how to really listen, the anger begins to dissipate and new possibilities emerge. A lack of listening isn't limited to hostile family members. In family meetings in general, it's a revelation to the parents to learn that their children feel that they have never been listened to, and it is a very positive experience for their children to feel that they have been listened to for the first time—either by their parents or by their siblings.

In some cases, anger is due to long-suppressed feelings. In one family, the three grown-up children—Charles, Karen and Randy— each ran a separate division of the company. At one meeting, Karen suddenly announced with unexpected bluntness and anger, "Randy, I don't think you're a good President—I think we should fire you!" Wham! This feeling had been stored up for years. The coach—one of our staff members—then said to Karen, "Okay, you've just said that Randy isn't a good president. What's the basis for that? What are your standards for being a good or a bad president?"

Karen replied, "Well, we've had three years of return-on-investment below that of the Dow-Jones industrials. My standard is at least to maintain the return above the DJ."

Then Randy answered the accusation. "There are extenuating circumstances. Our industry is in a slump—you know that." He continued by citing problems with other companies with similar products.

Karen said, "That's just an excuse. I still think you should resign."

We then helped the three of them work together to establish observable and measurable standards for their performance—not only Randy's performance, but the performance of each of them. Then each one was asked to approve these standards. Not only that, but each one agreed to resign if they didn't meet these standards. Copies of this agreement were then sent to the Boards of Directors of each division. It was important for the coach not to inject his own opinions but to allow them to determine their own standards.

Hostile family members, or amiable family members who have suppressed their feelings, find a safer forum in the family meeting. While Mom and Dad are still in charge of the meeting, the atmosphere created by the family coach makes it all right for younger and grown-up children to express personal values and beliefs, and to test Mom's and Dad's beliefs because they are testing them not as their children but as formal participants of the meeting.

This is a forum where touchy subjects can be discussed. For example, if a son and his wife need more money and want to sell some of their stock, they have to understand that it is going to decrease their capital, which means a permanent decrease in earning power. Everyone needs to understand that over the long term a considerable amount of potential income will be lost by selling shares now. The active participation of all family members allows the grown-up children and their spouses to understand and consider all their options—it is a conversation about possibilities.In addition to the currently-participating members of the family, we recommend that the entrepreneur of the family select people outside of the family who will act as advisers to the family if he or she dies. This advisory group worked well in the case of Peggy Fletcher. Peggy's husband, Brad, had been ill for three years before he died. During those last three years he had neglected the business and, at the time of his death, the company was in deep trouble with three million dollars of debt obligations. The debt was burying it. Peggy called me one day and said, "Roy, I'm in trouble. My lawyer and my accountant say I have to file for bankruptcy. I need your help." On the next Saturday morning, when I arrived at her home, several other businessmen, whom I knew, were also there. We worked all day on finding ways to get around bankruptcy. When we were finished, Peggy had a plan to save the company. Later, I wondered if my wife would have had the presence to call for help and, if so, whom would she have called, and would they be the same ones I would recommend? From that day forward, I have made sure that competent crisis advisers are available in my own family, and we recommend that each of our clients do the same.

For each family with whom we work, we recommend a number of crisis advisers, each with an experience that can be brought to bear if needed in the future. The most important thing about these advisers is that they should be persons who have gained your family's trust. You need to be able to trust in their integrity, their common sense and, when they don't know something, their ability to find the right answers. At least once a year, all of these crisis advisers should attend a family meeting so that your spouse and children can get to know them and feel comfortable with them as well.

Family meetings are typically called once a quarter for the first few years. After that, the frequency may slow to about twice a year, depending on the needs of the particular family. Once each year (more or less, depending on the specific needs of a family) there is a special meeting. The entire family and all advisers should attend this special meeting, as well as key executives of the business. Each executive delivers a state-of-the-business report for his area of responsibility, and the business owner gives a summary of it all. In this way, the professional advisers know what's going on and can do their jobs better, and the spouse and children get to see more aspects of the often-mysterious world of the family business and other assets.

When a family sits down together at a meeting, no family-related subject is off limits. The daughter may bitterly resent Dad and Mom's willingness to pay for her MBA but their refusal to give her a penny for acting school. Or Mom may see Dad's health declining and be terribly worried because he won't let up on his business schedule. When these kinds of subjects come up, the conversaton can get heated. And because Dad is usually the strong, assertive, entrepreneurial type, he dominates the discussions and the other family members may be intimidated.

Here is where an objective intermediary—the family coach—is of real help. A coach is someone who not only has the experience to help the family plan for the transfer of their wealth, but who also has the skills and sensitivity to guide the family communication process in a productive direction. Part of the coach's effectiveness is that he can't be bullied; he has the credentials, the authority and the experience (as well as the family's permission) to keep the meeting moving in a positive direction. Another advantage is his objectivity. Often, family members are so emotionally involved that they lose sight of what they are trying to accomplish; the coach keeps things on track.

A skilled coach can hear things that slip by family members. Frequently, Mom or Dad will give opinions out of long habit, without really believing what they are saying. The coach may then ask other family members to give feedback on what they have just heard. When they have given their view on what Mom or Dad has said, the coach will ask Mom or Dad, "Does that accurately reflect what you intended to convey? Is that what you really feel?" It often turns out that Mom or Dad has been avoiding a difficult issue. Dad may be having problems with the business that are taking a lot of his time and energy, or he may be having difficulties with his wife, children or grandchildren. When this is the case, it's hard to get him to focus on this issue that he's managed to sweep under the rug for years.

The carefully elicited feedback from family members about what other family members have said eliminates ambiguities. No one can say, at a later time, "That isn't what you said!"

Some subjects can be painful. In one family, the father made a judgment call that skirted the edge of good ethics. His sons called him on it and wanted a thorough airing of the matter. Dad resisted strongly until the coach finally said to him, privately, "This is creating a problem. If you don't face it, this issue will haunt you for the rest of your life and your sons will distrust you from now on." As is most often the case, once the issue was brought out on the table, it wasn't nearly as serious as either the sons or Dad had imagined it, and the whole problem was resolved.

Sometimes, as coaches, we speak privately to each family member about a particular subject before it is brought up in a family meeting. This prepares them for it, and defensive reactions have a chance to cool down. Because the coach is often the one who, however tactfully, introduces a subject and forces the family to address it, he is often the scapegoat. We've borne the wrath of strong-willed male and female entrepreneurs many times, but it's worth being the "bad guy" when the benefits are so impressive. Invariably, when family members work through a painful but necessary discussion with the aid of a coach, they become closer when it is finished.

Usually, it is the children who have a hard time bringing up delicate subjects with their parents, but sometimes it is the other way around. A recent example is Stanley and Wilma Ehrlich. The Ehrlichs have a substantial estate and they want to pass it on through their bloodline. That is, they don't want sons-in-law or daughters-in-law to be inheritors. What they want to avoid is having money leave their bloodline if there is a divorce some time in the future. They were afraid to bring up this issue because they didn't want to hurt anyone's feelings or disrupt their grown-up childrens' marriages. We were able to help because we are always coming from a neutral position and can raise an issue without being accused of favoritism.

In another meeting with the Ehrlich family, we discussed distributing their wealth among four grown-up children, all of whom were married. There was potential for conflict here. One of the sons had done several things to embarrass the family, and he was known to be flighty and unrealistic. Stanley was very apprehensive about letting him have any control over substantial parts of their assets. We began by handing out copies of a list of definitions of competence levels. This list described various levels of competence from beginning to highly-skilled levels. Then we listed, on an easel pad, the areas where family members were concerned about competence. These areas included such things as money management, property management, requirements for being the company President or any other position of employment, succession planning, as well as personal areas such as parent-child relations. For each of these areas of concern, we asked all family members to evaluate their own skill levels.

In a situation like this, no one addresses the less capable, less respected individual and says, "You are incompetent." On the contrary, each family member reads the descriptions for the different levels of competence and chooses the level which most closely corresponds to his or her own skills. Because there is no external criticism or other pressure being placed on them, the participants tend to evaluate themselves honestly and fairly.

In this way, the less competent individual can be candid about himself while still maintaining the "cover" of an abstract discussion. In the process, the other members of the family learn how he wants to be treated. The less competent individual will usually acknowledge that his role in the control of family wealth should not necessarily be the same as the other siblings, as long as he has some kind of role.

Because all of this has been brought out into the open, the family's perceptions begin to change. The black sheep is no longer quite so black and is no longer automatically labeled as incompetent. Now he seems more like someone who is special and who can make some kind of acceptable contribution to the family. And, in fact, he almost invariably can. It may not be in the area of business and finance—his contribution may be in other areas that haven't been explored. One of our functions as coaches is to help the family create some kind of contributing role which allows the less capable individual some dignity and helps to build his confidence. The result is, in spite of his limitations, he is starting to be perceived as part of the team instead of as an obstacle. It is a win-win situation.

Sometimes the entrepreneur of the family is so close to a situation he can't see that he is caught in a pattern of repeating errors. Then the job of the coach is to point this out to him. This happened with David Meltzer, who owns a company on the West Coast. Dave, together with his brother and sister, inherited equal shares of the business. Dave ran the business; his brother and sister weren't involved. When Dave turned 60, the brother and sister wanted to cash out and they forced him to sell the company. Dave was angry and felt betrayed after the many years he'd spent building it up. After the sale, Dave picked himself up again and started a new company with his oldest son. When I met Dave, the company was doing several million dollars in annual sales after only two years, so it had grown rapidly.

In addition to his son, who helps run the company, Dave has a younger son and a daughter. When I asked him how much of the company he owned, he said, "I own two-thirds and my son owns one-third; I put up the capital and he put up the sweat equity." I then asked him what he was going to do with his two-thirds, and he said, "Give it to my other two kids." Then I said, "Dave, do you realize what you're setting up? You just told me a few hours ago how angry you were with your brother and sister, and now you're telling me you're going to do the same thing with your kids?"

Dave was dumbfounded. Until that moment, this sharp, highly talented businessman was totally unaware that he had set the stage for a repetition of the same kind of sibling bitterness he, himself, had experienced.

Sometimes, problems which seem intractable to family members prove relatively easy to solve with the aid of a coach. A story about a business owner of long ago illustrates this nicely. This particular businessman was in transportation—specifically, camels. He had reached a point in his life where he was ready to turn his business over to his three sons. His assets were seventeen camels.

His oldest son was diligent and dutiful, so the businessman set aside half his camels for him. His second son, though not so diligent, was nevertheless creative and thoughtful. He got one-third of the camels. The youngest son never took anything seriously and was likely to squander his inheritance, so the father set aside only a ninth portion for him.

The businessman had a succession plan drawn up for him by his legal advisers and then picked an auspicious day for the transfer of his wealth. When the day approached, he thought about his seventeen camels and suddenly realized he had made a terrible mistake. With seventeen camels, it was impossible to divide them into half, third and ninth portions. But his legal advisers told him the succession plan was binding and must go through.

Having heard of a wise man, he went to see him and explained his problem. The wise man told him not to worry—that he would take care of the problem on the day of the succession. When that day arrived, the three sons were busy counting the camels they were to receive, scratching their heads and arguing bitterly. Their father waited anxiously until the wise man arrived. Curiously, the wise man, himself, was leading a camel.

"Greetings," said the wise man, I have brought you my camel. I will give him to you for the next few minutes and that will solve your problem." The father, now more anxious than ever, groaned and asked, "How can that possibly solve my problem?" "Notice," said the wise man, that you now own eighteen camels. Half of them is nine. Give nine camels to your oldest son. One-third of your eighteen camels is six. Give six camels to your middle son. A ninth portion of your eighteen camels is two. Give two camels to your youngest son. You have now fulfilled your pledge to your sons, and you have given away seventeen of your eighteen camels. Now give me back the eighteenth camel and the job is done."

This coach had made a difference.

While Dad, as the entrepreneur, is the information source regarding the business, and the coach offers insight and guidance, Mom and the children also have an important role to play in family meetings when they act as Chairman. They may be uncomfortable as Chairman because they are unused to dealing with professional authority figures. It is a new experience for them to call everyone to order, including lawyers, executives and other advisers that may be present. Also, some wives and (or husbands) are so habituated to allowing their spouses to take the lead in public, especially in matters pertaining to business, that it is hard for them to take control of the meeting in the presence of their spouse.

Mom is actually highly qualified to chair these meetings. She has been mediating for the family for years, even though she hasn't done it formally. She is so used to instinctively dealing with the family that she doesn't realize how effective she is. After a while, Mom will start to realize that even though the meeting proceedings are formal, she is basically doing the same thing she already does every day with her husband and children. As she becomes more accustomed to her role, Mom brings into play all of her subtle social skills: sensing when to press for something and when to back off; knowing how to give encouragement when it is needed; detecting when someone is disingenuous; and being able to make use of the strengths and weaknesses of each member of the family.

While Mom or one of the children is acting as Chairman at any particular family meeting, Dad is still a powerful participant. But he is only a participant—not the sole decision-maker. Mom's and the childrens' chairing of the family meetings is by no means an idle pursuit. They are getting practice at what they may have to do in the future. If Dad should suddenly die, they will be more competent and more comfortable in dealing with professional advisers and business executives. Also, in this role, Mom and the children will learn how and when to bring in consultants if additional information is needed in order to make decisions.

Young children also make real contributions to family meetings. When your children are still young—nine or ten years old—or later on, when your grandchildren are around that age, try taking them with you to business meetings. Even if they just sit there like little mice, the complexion of the meeting is changed. The adults not only use cleaner, more careful language, they go to great lengths to explain things clearly. The whole atmosphere of the meeting is lighter and more pleasant. Of course, you don't want to include small children all the time, but it's both fun and rewarding to do it when appropriate.

Children are also good at picking up the feelings, moods and attitudes of adults in a group. Sometimes when an adviser reports to a family, one of the children may later say that they are uncomfortable with that person. This can be a great time for the family to learn more about trust, and to discuss the basis for trusting or not trusting. Many times, a child will detect insincerity. If the family agrees with this perception, it may be appropriate to replace the adviser or at least make him or her aware of the breakdown in trust, and provide an opportunity to improve it. The most important issue here is not only for children to listen to opinions, but to judge their credence. This will enhance the children's confidence in their own perceptions and their ability to express them.

Having children occasionally sit in on business meetings gives them a new perspective on what really happens in these meetings. If they have been influenced by peers who have anti-business views, who believe businessmen are dishonest or that they are only interested in taking advantage of people, these meetings will help them see that managing a business is hard work, and work which demands a high level of integrity and ethical standards.

When young adults are able to participate in family meetings, and learn to chair a meeting—not just trying it once as a novelty, but long enough to develop skill at controlling the meeting, it is immediately apparent what a dynamite idea it is and what confidence it gives these young adults.

Sometimes, in a family meeting, when Dad dominates it in spite of Mom's position as Chairman, the grown-up children are able to work together to push through a decision that is right. This happened to Jim Weygand's family, where there were three sons and one daughter. Toward the end of the meeting, Jim suddenly announced that he had chosen his oldest son, Evan, to become President of the company. The company was an automobile parts distributorship. After Jim's announcement, the whole room became silent. It was a surprise to everyone, including Mom and two of Jim's closest advisers. Evan, the subject of the announcement, didn't look pleased either.

After a moment, Evan said, very tentatively, "Look, Pop, Lucie is really the most capable executive. I think she should be President." Jim got angry at that and shouted, "No way. I'm not going to have a girl President. Besides, Lucie doesn't want to be President." Then things began to get heated, but the presence of the coach enabled everyone to speak their mind. When Lucie, got a chance to talk, she was calm but very firm: "Pop, you never asked me. You asked all of the boys if they were interested but you never once mentioned the possibility to me. Well now you know. I do want to be president."

Jim didn't cave in all at once on this issue. Lucie's desire to be President was as much a shock to him as his announcement had been to the family. To his credit, he retreated graciously by saying he'd have to think about it until the next family meeting, three months later. During that time, everyone worked on persuading him. His wife, Susan, plus all four siblings coaxed him. At the next meeting Jim agreed that Lucie was the best choice for President, and everyone was pleased. It was another win-win situation.

This particular event is an example of how grown-up children can become empowered. Not only does their collective wisdom often result in good decisions, they also learn the value of mutual support, of standing together for a good cause.

After a family meeting has ended, and all non-family members have left, the coach asks the entire family to have a debriefing session. We strongly encourage them to do this without the coach present. In this way, they can freely discuss our input and our role in the meeting, and our observations. We want the family to talk about what happened at the meeting; what was actually said and what was meant between the lines. Dad, as the business expert, or Mom, as the case may be, will explain business issues to the rest of the family. Because there may have been other issues involved, including personal matters, it is important that each family member be able to share his or her observations. We also ask the family to discuss each participant's contribution to the meeting.

This debriefing session benefits everyone. The family begins to understand that advisers advise and that executives are the ones who execute, or implement, decisions. In observing and evaluating the give-and-take between the coach and the family advisers, the family will start to see the specialized focus of the family advisers and why, by definition, their roles are limited.

During the debriefing, the Chairman reviews the observable and measurable standards that were established at the outset of the meeting. Did the meeting accomplish what the family desired? If not, why not?

The Chairman then makes up an action list—the steps the family will take as a result of this meeting. If further information is needed to undertake an action, that's okay, but acquiring the necessary information must become one of the action steps. The point is, the family shouldn't drift back to the status quo as a result of the meeting, but should spell out specific actions to be taken, who is responsible for implementing them, and on what timetable.

The feedback we receive from family members after we've concluded family meetings is very satisfying. Here's an example from a young adult, the son of an entreprenmeur.

"I think we covered a lot. Parts of it were tough, but, overall, it was very positive. I have a better feeling of where we're going with the Trust. The pact we made about gossip and that we would not say anything about a person except to them directly was very important to me. I learned that to make all this work, to make the Trust work, we will need communication skills.

"This has given me a great opportunity to understand my parents. My respect for them is greater. I believe I have more confidence to discuss things from what I learned in this meeting. I learned that it was important to ask questions. I felt honesty and sincerity and interest from everyone in contributing to the family group—specifically about the family Trust. I'd been wanting something like this to happen for a long time.

"I'm learning how breakdowns in conversations happen. I've learned some new tools. At first I didn't see why we needed a coach, but now I recognize his role and I hope he'll continue to be involved with us in the future.

"I'm pleased with our creating a family mission statement. I feel better and more confident. I feel like an integral part of the family. It was an incredible, wonderful two days. I'm glad we did it."

There are a great many benefits derived from family meetings. Some of the major ones are:

- Provide a forum to discuss family issues in safety
- Allow sensitive and taboo subjects to be aired
- Learn to use the tools of effective communication
- Build bridges of trust between all family members, including in-laws
- Enable all family members to learn more about the family business
- Teach the grown-up children how to deal with family advisers
- Enable the entrepreneur's spouse to learn more about the business and to participate in decison-making
- Establish measurable and observable standards of competency of family members in all areas that affect the family
- Establish teams to work together on family tasks in-between family meetings
- Enable all family members to have some role in the family team

Many of the things I have mentioned in this chapter about family meetings, while powerful, may seem rather simple. After all, aren't they mostly based on common sense, and shouldn't intelligent family members be able to apply common sense by themselves and get the same results? So why bother with a family coach and formal meetings?

After decades of experience along these lines, the answer is unequivocal. The biases, buried resentments, fears and established behavior patterns among family members are so ingrained that it is extremely difficult for a family to work these out by themselves; it requires much experience and sensitivity to channel all of these diverse feelings and desires into a common purpose. When this is coupled with the need for a broad expertise in preparing heirs for succession and effective estate planning, it is almost impossible for families to undertake this process without a skilled coach.

But, with the right kind of assistance, the family meeting is a very, very powerful tool. It gives a strong boost to bringing the family closer together, in defining family goals and in seeing those goals accomplished.

4 Introducing Your Business Self to Your Family

| Preparing Heirs | Trust and Communication | Estate/Succession Planning |

With the powerful tool of family meetings, we have made more progress in the climb up our pyramid. In this chapter I will begin by asking you what a friend asked me over lunch, twenty years ago. Here's what he asked me: "Why are you in the business you are in today?" At first it seemed to be a simple question that deserved an equally simple answer. But, as I began to think about it, I decided I needed a bit more time. So I replied, "I'll call you by 4:00 this afternoon and give you my answer." When I started reflecting on it, first my family came to mind, and I thought: "It's for my family—I'm in business to build a future for my family." That was an element, of course, but as I continued to ponder it, I felt that that was not the essential reason. As I asked myself the question over and over, other questions came to mind: "Am I in business to build a basis for comfortable retirement? Am I doing it to leave something tangible behind in the world? Is it for the challenge of the chase? Is it because I want to pursue my own ideas, and for that reason I won't work for anyone else? Or has it simply become a routine that I do, whose only motive is that it is easier to keep doing it than to stop?"

The more I thought about why I was really in business, the more the question bothered me. When 4:00 p.m. came, I called my friend and said, "I don't have a good answer yet, but when I do, I'll call you." I'm sure I heard a soft chuckle as he hung up.

Weeks went by, then a month. I would wake up at two or three in the morning with a new idea that was only part of the answer. The trouble was, there was an element of truth in all of my answers but none was the essential reason. It took me months of reflecting to finally understand why I was really in business.

Six months after he had asked me, I telephoned my friend. I finally realized that the thing that really put passion into my work, what really provided fulfillment, was working to improve the lives of my clients and their families, and to be able to see the beneficial results. That is the essential reason why I am in business, the driving force behind the long hours and hard work. I also realized that in order to continue to help my clients I must be able to stay in business, and to be able to stay in business I must make a profit, and to make a profit I must put my time and energy into my business—it won't do it by itself. So I know why I am in business.

Now I am passing the question on to you. Why are you in business today? Why are you engaged in accumulating wealth? Is it for your family? Is it because you enjoy the day-to-day operations? Is it the challenge of competition? What is the purpose of all the energy and creativity which you give to your wealth-producing activity? This activity is something to which you're giving the lion's share of the hours of each week, almost every week of your life. Why?

It's not only important to know the answer for yourself, but for your children to know it as well. Often, children, when they are growing up, get a mistaken impression of the family business because they hear only the negative details that Dad or Mom voice to let off steam. Many children are asking: "What does our family business contribute to the world that is worthwhile?" They don't understand all of the positive aspects of the business you take for granted because you are so involved with it. Often, even when they are grown-up, your children don't realize the impact of the business on the lives of your employees, on the businesses of your suppliers and on the welfare of your customers.

How can you expect young adults to get fired up about being a part of the business if they don't really have an understanding of its impact? How can they make intelligent decisions about whether or not to get involved until they know something about it, and the reasons for its existence?

A good place to start is to tell your children about how and why you first started the business. When we coach at family meetings, we invite Dad to tell how the business got started. We ask questions such as: What was the original reason for starting the business? How did Dad select the industry? Was it hard to get started? Were there times when he thought he might not make it? Did he ever doubt himself?

We'll invite Dad to be candid about his own shortcomings. When did he guess wrong? What were some of his major mistakes? An example comes to mind in the life of Sam Nomura, and a substantial mistake he made that nearly ruined him.

At a family meeting with Sam, his wife, Connie, and their two boys, I said, "Sam, would you care to tell the boys about the time when your Dad let you buy some property, and what happened after that." Sam groaned and said, "Ouch! It still hurts to remember that. It was over twenty years ago, and I came real close to going belly-up.

"I wanted to buy 700 acres and my Dad put up the down payment and arranged the financing. I wanted to build a real nice subdivision. You know, wide streets, recreation center, three and four bedroom houses with large family rooms. Good quality construction. They were gonna go for $100,000—this was 1965. Well, I had sold a few houses but just as the work was almost completed, interest rates went through the roof and there was a housing slump...not just here, but all over the country.

"On top of that, I was overextended, trying to do too much with the money I had available. Well, I was scared, real scared. I didn't think I could meet payroll, and my suppliers...I felt awful about making them wait, but I just couldn't pay them. I went to the banks and tried to get additional financing. They kept telling me, 'You can't do it. You're not going to make it.' I was very angry at these guys, and I remember telling them, 'I am going to make it!' But all I got back was, 'Not with our money you're not.' "

By this point in the family meeting, Sam's sons were all ears. Even his wife, Connie, hadn't realized how difficult that period had been for her husband. They all wanted to know how he got out of it, and Sam continued: "I worked my tail off, even poured concrete myself. I sold off some lots to get cash for payroll. And I won't say I lied outright to the banks, but I sure stretched the truth. I finally got a bit more money out of them, and things started to turn around. I sold a few more houses and finally managed to pay off the suppliers. Then the market picked up again. But for a while, it was real close.

"The truth is I overextended myself and I should have set up additional credit lines for contingencies—but I didn't, and I learned."

In another case, Hugh Porter, who was in the oil-drilling business, was in the process of turning over his business to his grown-up children when there was suddenly an opportunity for a deal, and Hugh went for it. We were at a family board meeting when Hugh told his wife and children: "I just lost most of your inheritance! It wasn't the lawyer's fault and it wasn't the accountant's fault. It was all me. My instinct told me there was something wrong but I ignored it. Kids, I really screwed up."

Although it was a substantial loss, this mistake brought the family closer together. As in Sam Nomura's case, until Hugh's children learned about some of the business errors their Father had made, they thought their Dad walked on water, and that he could do no wrong. These meetings, where Dad opens up and tells about his errors, are real eye-openers. What extraordinarily powerful lessons! Dad says, "I screwed up. I accept the responsibility. It wasn't anyone else's fault—it was my fault." That's teaching the children accountability. It's teaching that it's okay to make mistakes and that, instead of blaming someone else for your mistakes, you admit them forthrightly and then you pick yourself up and try again.

In Hugh porter's case, he and his children have worked together to more than make up that loss. In the long run, that episode will turn out to be a plus for the family.

The image many sons and daughters have of their fathers is invincibility. Dad's perfect—they can never measure up to or equal

Dad because they're human and he isn't. So when you acknowl-edge your mistakes and you admit to some of the human emo-tions of feeling guilty, depressed or culpable about having made them, your children see that you are human and vulnerable. This starts to build a climate of safety and trust within the family in which your children can be free to say anything. By seeing your vulnerability, you are letting your children know that it's okay if they make mistakes—nobody's perfect. And by showing that you, too, have real feelings, that you have problems you are concerned about, you're letting them know that you are human, just as they are.

Parents feel that they need to be strong for their children, and most of the time that's warranted. After all, you've been safeguard-ing your kids since they were born. That means the energy has always been flowing one way—from you to them. By demonstrat-ing to them your shortcomings and your vulnerability, you are, for the first time, allowing a bit of that energy to flow back to you. And when you have shown them that you, too, need love, sup-port, encouragement and, sometimes, even sympathy, you'll be creating the strong family bonds that are worth more than mil-lions.

At family meetings we also ask Dad what important values he has instilled in the business. Is integrity an important principle in the company's operations? How about always being honest with the customer—even when it hurts? Does the company value and care about its employees? Are these values upheld throughout the company, and do the executives believe in them? If not, could it be because Dad, himself, does not set an example for the values he espouses? And if not, is it due to inattention or does Dad, him-self, not really believe in these values? If Dad does believe in them, but they have been allowed to lapse within the company, is Dad open to reestablishing them? These are important points because, to the young or grown-up children, their degree of trust and their interest in participating in the family business will be strongly in-fluenced by whether or not Dad actually lives his values—or at least attempts to.

We don't ask Dad to speak only of shortcomings, of course. We encourage him to tell the children what he is most proud of in the business. Has he managed to bring his executives to a high level of competence? Has he created a widget that improves peoples' lives? Has he captured market share against larger, richer companies? Does he receive positive feedback from satisfied customers? Has the company shown a profit even during lean times?

Now that your grown-up children have been exposed to some of your values, some of your shortcomings and some of your accomplishments—now that they know you are human—it's time to broaden that impression and involve them further by sharing your goals with them. Where are you taking the business? Is your primary goal to increase sales to a higher figure, or is it to capture market share? Or is your main goal to produce the finest quality product in your industry? Sam Nomura, the real estate developer, is very clear to his kids about his goal. He wants to build one of the most beautiful, planned-unit developments in California and make a profit at the same time. He's enthusiastic and excited about it. Sam's two sons are caught up in the challenge, and they're working hard at it. Sam is pleased the three of them not only share this goal but, together, are setting new ones all the time.

Sharing your business and investment goals with your family means more than merely stating them. It means letting your children feel they are a part of the picture by telling them the risks involved and the challenges that must be overcome in order to meet your goals. It means listening to their opinions about the best way to reach these goals, and, also, their opinions about the importance of the goals, themselves.

And sharing your goals also means letting your children feel your excitement about the challenge of using assets effectively and wisely.

The title of this chapter is, "Introducing Your Business Self To Your Family," but as I have said earlier, by business I mean to include all family investments, philanthropy, estate management activities, etc. So what I have meant to convey in this chapter is that it is important for you to introduce your family to your business and financial self. Share with the children how you got started and the problems you've overcome. By doing this you are revealing a great deal about what makes you tick. No matter what else you do, this sharing of yourself will bring dividends over and over again in closer family ties, and you will become a better role model for your grown-up children to do the same for their children.

5 How Your Business Affects Your Family

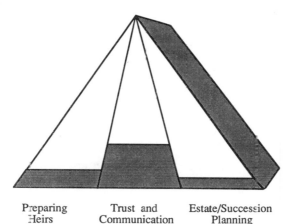

| Preparing Heirs | Trust and Communication | Estate/Succession Planning |

You are probably the most influential role model your children will ever know. It would be hard to overestimate your effect on them, an effect that will last throughout their lives. Sherry X., who inherited a furniture store, recalls her experience: "My parents often talked about values—that I should always be honest, never steal or cheat, and that I should heed the Golden Rule. As far as I could tell, when I was growing up, they were honest and formally polite—I mean, they never shouted or used bad language. But as I got older, I began to realize that they didn't really live their values.

"I remember they hired furniture movers for six months and then fired them and rehired new people so they wouldn't have to pay wages of fifty cents more per hour. And when one of the movers got hurt from moving a heavy bed frame, they fought him in court to get out of paying for the part of the medical bills that the state didn't cover.

"At home, Mom told me about the charities they were donating to, but then I watched my Mom call the maid to come from another part of the house to pick up something from the floor that she could just have bent over and gotten herself. And when we were having a dinner party, Dad would make the cook stay late after she'd worked all day, even though Mom and Dad knew she had four small children at home to take care of.

"So I gradually started to realize that Mom and Dad weren't living the values they talked about. Oh, they never did anything illegal, but they were totally insensitive to the welfare of others. After that, I stopped trusting them. To this day I still don't trust them. I mean, they're my Mom and Dad, and I love them and I appreciate what they've done for me, but I don't trust them. The worst thing about it is that once in a while, in spite of my knowing better, I find myself doing the same things they do, and then I just hate myself."[1]

Your children are generally more aware of the negative effects of role modeling than the positive ones. But the positive effects of role-modeling can be a powerful influence as well. An acquaintance of mine in the publishing business tells this story about how his Father affected him.

"I grew up in Chicago during the years of World War II. Things were scarce then, and food was rationed. But in the midst of these scarcities, our family was fortunate because my Father had a wholesale food business and we were able to get just about everything edible. Everyone liked my Dad—he had friends everywhere, and he knew how to treat them.

"I got a good glimpse of how that worked one day, as well as how the city of Chicago worked. That day I was riding in my Dad's truck, helping to deliver some large wheels of hard-to-get Wisconsin cheddar cheese to some posh restaurants. The downtown section of Chicago known as 'The Loop' was, even then, a very crowded area. It was almost impossible to find a parking place.

"At that time, all of the downtown traffic police rode horses, and spent most of their time handing out parking tickets to the illegally parked cars and trucks. We double-parked our truck in front of the restaurant and, before making the delivery, my Dad took a big knife and cut a wedge out of one of the cheese wheels and wrapped it up. Those cheese wheels were really big—about 90 lbs. each—and that one wedge weighed almost 20 lbs. My Dad told me it was for one of the cops (that's what they called them-selves—never 'police officers') who was having a hard time mak-ing ends meet.

"Moments later I heard the clip-clop of hooves on pavement, and a burly, middle-aged cop came up to our truck and leaned over into the cab. He called out, 'Hi, Carl, hawaya? That your sonny boy with you?' I waved to the cop and, after the mutual inquiries about families were over, my Dad said, 'Mike, I'm overloaded with too much cheese this week, and it's only going to waste. Could you help me out by taking some off my hands?' and he handed over that big wedge of cheese. The cop's eyes lit up over that, and he stuck the cheese into his saddlebag, two-thirds of it sticking out like a bright orange tower.

"After thanking my dad, the cop asked, 'Delivering today, Carl?' My Dad told him yes and the cop said, 'Just leave the truck here and I'll direct traffic around you.' I helped my Dad carry in two cheese wheels and when we came back outside, there was the cop, seated on his tall brown horse, making a detour for the traffic until my Dad could move our truck out of the way. That was how Chicago worked in those days. It wasn't exactly bribery or pay-off—I sensed the cop would have helped my Dad even without the gift of cheese. But though I was just a young boy, I remember being impressed by my Father's thoughtfulness, not only in giv-ing, but in the way he had given so that the cop lost no dignity in receiving.

"In all of his business dealings, my Dad was a wonderful role model. And where most of us count ourselves fortunate to have a few really close friends, my Dad had them by the dozens—per-sons who would do anything for him, and vice versa. I've tried to do the same thing with my employees, with my associates and with my own son and daughter. I owe my Dad a large debt of gratitude, and I think of him often as I try to be as positive an influence on my children as he was to me."

Part of the role model you present to your children comes from your own self-image. And while your own self-image should be based on what you think of yourself as a whole person, often it is not.

Some Dads and Moms have a self-image that is based on their net worth. When a self-image is based on possessions, that person may talk about himself in terms of how many houses he owns, and the value of his company and investments. With others, their self-image comes from their title as CEO. When self-image is based on a title, that individual may think of himself in terms of his role as money-maker. Although a self-image like this may not be bluntly voiced, you are still subconsciously broadcasting it to your children: "The more money I make, the more possessions I own or the more prestigious my title, the more important and powerful I am." Of course, the flip side to that is if you should lose some or all of your assets, you have then become less important and weaker.

As your children grow up, they see the use of money and power as a way of solving problems. They observe how their parents use money to impact business, political and personal needs. From watching this over the years, they can easily assume that money and power are necessary in order to be important.

When your children become adults and see that your image of self-worth is based, for example, on your title as Chief Executive Officer or Chief Financial Officer, what happens to the young men and women who can't reach these top levels? They may end up feeling that they're not worth anything. This happened in Don Penning's family, where Don had three sons, and spent years telling them how great it was to be CEO, how owning and controlling your own company was the only way to go. Don was so wrapped up in his self-image as CEO that it never occurred to him what he was doing to his sons. He chose one of them to take over as CEO, and the other two sons elected to take jobs with other companies. Even though these young men both have leadership ability and even though they're advancing as executives, they live with the constant feeling that they don't measure up. They know, from Dad, that being on the top is all that counts, and that their brother has succeeded and they haven't.

Role modeling covers every aspect of life. Who sees the affection between you and your wife, or the lack of it? Who watches how you treat relatives, friends, associates and even strangers? Who is aware, from your casual comments at home, of whether or not you bring integrity to your business deals? And who senses if you are fair or unfair, kind or cruel, honest or dishonest, generous or selfish? Your children notice all of this. And, by and large, they won't live the way you tell them to live—they'll live the way you live. Of all the assets you can leave your children, none is more precious than the role model you provide for them.

Another major factor in guiding your sons and daughters is to create a healthy relationship between them and the family assets. This means understanding that wealth is a part of the family. And, just as women give birth to children, entrepreneurs, both male and female, beget wealth. In the majority of cases, the entrepreneur sees the development of wealth in somewhat the same way that a mother experiences the birth and growth of her children. In this sense, the wealth that has been built up is a member of the family, and the children are brothers and sisters to it.

Most of us try to treat our sons and daughters with equal love and attention, and not play favorites. We realize that each child has his or her strengths and weaknesses, and we try not to favor one over the other. So, if family assets are just one more brother or sister in the family, why does Dad lavish so much time and attention on them? It's because wealth-production is the "kid" that gives the most back to Dad. He gets all of his strokes from it. And where we get our strokes is where we spend our time.

Do the rest of the family members notice? You bet they do. They know who Dad's favorite "kid" is. Many wives look upon the business as a mistress. And the children have every right to react just like brothers and sisters do when they feel that their parents love one sibling more than another.

It's natural for Dad to get so involved in the business that it eats up most of his time. But this sends the family a double message: Dad professes to love the family first, but what the kids see is, "My brother, the business, is what Dad loves most." And the moment you have that, your children start to get jealous of the business sibling who is getting all the attention.

Some possible fallout of this is when your daughter's actions say, "I couldn't get you to come to my ballet recital, Dad, but I know I'll get your attention if I get pregnant." Or with your son's involvement with drugs: "You missed my basketball game again, Dad, but if I'm doing dope I'll bet you notice."

Most business owners with families have conflicting goals: spend time with the business or spend time with the family. The owner is frequently under stress because he always seems to be neglecting one for the other. So how important is your family to you?

In all of my thirty-plus years of practice, only once did I come across someone—I'll call him Monty—who came right out and said, "Money is more important." Monty's family was untrusting; there was a lot of bitter squabbling going on, and they kept pressuring him until he finally hired us. During the course of our working together, Monty admitted that every time he wrote us a check for our services, his stomach did a flip-flop and he became angry. He had been an orphan, and grew up feeling unwanted and unimportant. As he grew up, the only thing that made him feel as though he was somebody was the accumulation of money. Every time he spent money—on anything—he felt diminished. After our second meeting, Monty announced that there weren't going to be any more family meetings. He openly announced to his wife and children that money was more important to him than they were. So he quit the process. His wife and children were devastated.

We can't do anything with someone like this. The Williams Group aren't psychologists and we can't change peoples' fundamental values; we can only help people clarify and strengthen and act upon their own values.

So an important part of our Integrated Wealth Transfer Process™ is to ask this fundamental question of our clients: "Which is more important to you—your family, or money, success and prestige?" Even if he's been working sixteen hours a day and rarely seeing his family, when it comes right down to it, essentially every entrepreneur will admit that his family is most important. Yet his actions seem to belie this.

I remember one of our clients—Phil Kronner—telling me how much he loved his wife and kids, and how important they were to him. I said, "Phil, you're telling me how important Jessie and the kids are to you, and yet you spend 90% of your time with the business and only 10% with them. Phil, something's out of balance."

Morris Blaisdell was a case in point. When we interviewed his daughter, Penny, she told us her dad was a very important businessman, that important politicians and business people often came to see him. She knew he was successful and that other people admired him, but she didn't trust him. I was incredulous. Others viewed Morris as a man of impeccable integrity—how could she say she didn't trust him? I asked her for a specific example and she said, "Last week I made an appointment to see him at 3:00 p.m. I arrived on time and sat in his office, waiting, until 6:00 p.m. Then his secretary came out and told me Dad was still in a board meeting and for me to go home. He would try to see me later in the evening.

The daughter said this had happened hundreds of times. It didn't take her long to figure out that business and money were more important to her dad than she was. I asked her if she had talked about this with Morris and she said, "Yes, many times, but he doesn't listen and he won't change."

At our next family meeting, we asked her to tell her Dad about her feelings of no trust, and she was brave—she did it. Morris listened but didn't really hear. Penny repeated it several times and he still didn't "hear" her. Finally, we held a listening exercise and, all of a sudden, a tear rolled down his cheek. Morris said, "Honey, I just did not know I was doing this. I'm building this company for you and your brothers and cousins. I was unaware of the impact my actions had on you." Morris then swore he would become the ultimate standard for reliability.

"I know you mean what you say right now, Daddy, but in three months you will do it again."

The next family meeting was set for the 4th of January. On December 10th I received a call from the President of the company, stating that the boss was changing the meeting date because he had a big deal going in South America during the first week in January.

I suggested to the President that this was not acceptable, and the President said, "You tell him—he signs my paychecks." We both laughed and then I called the owner. He restated why he was changing the meeting date. I told him this was not acceptable. Suddenly, his voice changed, and he put on his owner's voice: why did I believe I had a basis for questioning him? I replied that it was not for me but for his promise to his daughter. What was more important, making more money or his reliability quotient with Penny?

"Oh, (expletive deleted)," was his reply, and he reaffirmed the original date of the family meeting—I'm sure at considerable expense and inconvenience, and the changing of many calendars.

On the 4th of January, Penny didn't show up for the family meeting; she had gone on a skiing trip. Morris was livid! At least until we pointed out that he would not have been there either, unless I had called him. After his initial anger, Morris started to take the whole problem more seriously. He asked, "How can I get at the root of this problem? How can I rebuild trust? I don't want this to continue to come between us."

In dealing with his family, Morris will have to become as rigorous as he is in business; every promise must be kept, every phone call returned, no cancellations except for emergencies. Our children emulate what we do, not what we say. Morris can gradually rebuild the trust he has lost, but it will take time.

Faced with a choice between business needs and family needs, most business owners opt for the business. Graduations are missed, family vacations get canceled, one-on-one time with the children is absent and the family hears a thousand excuses for why Dad isn't there. Dad knows that he's been neglecting his children, and they know it too. Although it may not be expressed, the family knows that the business gets a higher priority than the family.

I once met a young lady on a plane. She had a darling baby that was just a few months old. I told her how excited I was with the birth of my own grandsons, and I mentioned how excited her father must be about her bringing the baby home for him to see for the first time. She said, "My father doesn't love the baby the way you are talking about. My father only loves with money. He bought the round-trip tickets for me to come, but I know he won't take the time to come to the airport." During the last 30 minutes of the flight, I begged her to share her feelings with her father, because he needed to hear her say that. He wouldn't like it, of course, but he needed to hear it.

After we had left the plane, I accompanied her to the outside arrivals area and waited with her for a while, still convinced that with a new baby her father would come. I was sure he would be there with open arms. After a while, a van pulled up with the company logo displayed on the door. A young man stepped out and took her luggage. She was right. Her father had sent the company deliveryman to pick her up.

This kind of perception, that Dad or Mom loves with money, is quite common. A son or daughter will say to us that Dad, in particular, doesn't know how to hug or show affection, he only loves with money when he feels guilty. Interestingly, they don't say this critically—it's a statement of fact, an acceptance of the way things are.

But behind the buying off of his children is Dad's neglect of them. This doesn't come from an intentional desire to neglect them, it arises because it is difficult for Dad to communicate or share activities with them. Faced with this difficulty, Dad turns to business challenges, which though complex, are more straightforward and emotionally easier for him to handle. Because the business provides for the family, overcoming business challenges instills a sense of duty in Dad. He feels that by spending so much time with the business he is really doing it for the family. In fact, in many cases, Dad has rationalized away his lack of ability to communicate with his kids and to be with them. And because he is more respected and generally gets more strokes at the business than with the family, Dad's sense of esteem and accomplishment are reinforced through the business.

This isn't a chapter on psychology or on how to get your children to love you. It's purpose is to encourage you to develop a better balance between your business and your children. If your grown-up children are going to take over the running of the business or if they will be responsible to some degree for managing family assets, someone has to start changing their perceptions of the role of the business and other assets in the family.

The essential requirement, in bringing the role of the business into better balance, is for Dad to spend more time with the family while the children are at home. The children need to know that the business need not be the all-demanding, all-consuming demon which steals all of Dad's time and energy. The family needs to know there is time for the kids, time for Mom, time to go camping, fishing, traveling or whatever they want to do together as a family. It doesn't have to be a lengthy trip. It may mean that, once in a while, Dad will spend an entire day with just one son or daughter.

This is an appropriate place to briefly mention the role of surrogate parents as part of the problem of imbalance. In her doctoral thesis, The Experience of Inherited Wealth: A Social-Psychological Perspective,[2] Joanie Bronfman reports on children of wealthy parents: "They described parents who were cold, distant, frequently absent, and who delegated much of the child-rearing to servants. These parents were often willing to relate to their children only on their own terms and they seemed more concerned that their children learned appropriate attitudes and behaviors than that they were well nurtured."

The same is true for modest income homes, especially where both parents work. Nurturing, when not left to baby sitters or older siblings, is increasingly the province of the TV.

Only later, when hindsight brings lost opportunities into focus, do many parents realize that they should have spent more time instilling values and building relations with their children.

Finding the appropriate balance between business and your family is not easy, and it requires a certain amount of discipline, delegating authority and planning ahead. When you're finalizing the figures for the annual report, trying to figure out the real cause of production delays and dealing with an employee lawsuit, it's hard to remember that your family needs your attention at home. It's a matter of priorities. But if you weren't already accomplished at juggling priorities, you'd never have been successful in business. What's needed, then, is to move your family up from the bottom of the priority list.

Part of your skill as a businessperson or manager of family assets is verifying that you have met certain goals or standards, and correcting things when you have not. The same thing applies to finding the time to spend with your family. Keep a record of some kind to periodically see how you're doing. Have you fulfilled all of your promises to your family? Probably not, but you're still a beginner at this. Remember the story I told about beginners in the Introduction, about my attempt to juggle silk scarves? As a beginner, you won't have a perfect record immediately—sometimes you'll fail. That's okay, but it's important to let your family know that you are trying, and that you want to work with them to rebuild their trust in you.

Ross Perot Jr. expressed the idea well in Fortune Magazine, when he talked about his famous father: "Kids have to know you've made them your No.1 priority. Even when Dad was busy traveling around the country on business, he would fly back to see us if we were in a school play. He always made sure we knew how special we were to him."[3]

Setting aside time for your children, and making that time inviolable, is one of the most effective ways to build family relationships and to instill positive values in your children. It is a high-yield investment.

1, 2 Bronfman, Joanie, Doctoral thesis, "The Experience Of Inherited Wealth: A Social-Psychological Perspective," UMI Dissertation Service, Ann Arbor, MI, 1987

3 *Fortune* magazine, September 10, 1990

6 Sharing Family Values

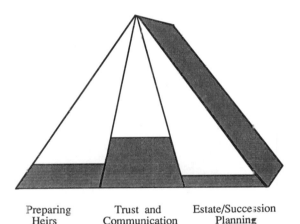

Preparing Heirs   Trust and Communication   Estate/Succession Planning

It often surprises us that family members who have spent a considerable part of a lifetime together really don't know each other. Time after time a husband, wife, daughter or son will say, "Gee, I didn't know you felt that way!" In our fast-paced lives we don't often have the opportunity to sit down with one another and really evaluate those fundamental values we hold dear. But it is those very values that will hold a family together or destroy it. This chapter is about your family members learning to share their personal values in order to discover common family values.

This process begins with the most basic relationship of the family—your marriage. The experiences of the McDowell family provide an example of how the quality of the marriage affects the family as a unit.

Hugh McDowell's family looked every bit the successful American dream. Married for 20 years, with three healthy, attractive children, a beautiful home with a 50-acre ranch, and a thriving loan brokerage business that Hugh had built up over the years. Two daughters and a son were in elementary and middle schools, and the children were about as well-behaved and balanced as children ought to be. Hugh and his wife, Emy, never fought and rarely disagreed. To all appearances, the McDowells lived in peace and harmony. They had more than adequate income, the kids seemed happy and were getting good grades in school, and both husband and wife appeared to be satisfied with their lives.

A closer look, however, showed that something was fundamentally wrong. Hugh spent most of his time at the office and, since Emy had domestic help at home, she was often absent as well, helping civic groups and the local theatrical association. In the few hours Hugh and Emy spent together at home, they didn't have much to say to each other or to the children. Hugh asked the kids a few obligatory questions about school and then ducked behind the newspaper.

Emy left meal preparation to the cook and, after making small talk with the children and formally kissing them, excused herself since she was needed at a staff meeting of the arts council.

It was all very polite and restrained. The children returned to their rooms, where each one had his own TV, VCR and computer. They spent most of their time at home in their rooms, and seldom played with each other.

This had been going on for several years. Hugh and Emy had separate lives and had gradually ceased talking to each other, except about perfunctory details of the household. All the family members were on parallel tracks—sharing the house and some of the routine of a family—while those tracks moved on without ever coming together. There was no real family. Hugh and Emy and the children had become roomers in a luxurious boarding house, each person seeking his or her own, private agenda.

Hugh first realized that something had to change when he began to think about a succession plan and a possible role for his children. After Hugh expressed interest in our program, we had had our first family meeting. It was obvious to me that a good deal of work on sharing needed to be done before tackling the problems of succession. Later, I met privately with Hugh in order to ask some personal questions. One of the questions I asked was, "Why are you married? I don't mean why you originally got married, I mean why you are married today?"

I didn't expect a quick answer, and it was a few months before we met again to discuss it. Hugh said he had thought about it quite a bit but had no simple answer. We discussed the point that marital trust and sharing is essential in order to have family trust and sharing. I then suggested that he and Emy do something they had not done for many years: go away together and spend an entire weekend or more to try to understand why they were married, and if there were sufficient reasons for them to continue to be married. It took some convincing, but they finally did it.

They stayed together for four days in a lodge at a beautiful resort area. Going along with my request, they agreed to remain in their room or take walks together—no distracting activities—until they had come up with some answers.

Those days were filled with strong emotions and not a few tears. In their particular case, Hugh and Emy's passive, mutual withdrawal had been precipitated by a marital problem that had erupted years before and had been swept under the rug. Over the years, they had deliberately built walls around themselves—walls that had prompted the children to emulate them by building their own walls.

During this intense weekend, Hugh and Emy were jolted out of their complacent separateness, and forced to look at themselves anew. What they saw made them both agree that they held many core values in common, and their marriage had a lot worth saving. They also agreed that there was much work to be done, and they committed themselves to tearing down the walls of separation.

A while later, at my suggestion, the McDowells agreed to a vacation that was unlike anything they'd ever done before. The idea was to make a certain amount of time and money available and, with as few restrictions as possible, let the children plan the vacation on their own. This meant deciding where to go, how to get there, arranging for travel tickets, tours and guides where necessary; changing money, researching weather conditions at their destination, and arranging for any required visas. It was a most extraordinary trip. Everyone did some things for the first time: Mom climbed her first mountain; Dad, for the first time in his marriage, sat back and allowed his wife and children tell him what to do; and the children did everything from ordering meals in foreign languages to zooming down a bobsled run (with experienced guides) at sixty miles per hour.

The vacation was an enormous success. When he told me about it after they had returned, Hugh was so proud of the competence his youngsters had exhibited that he was about to burst. He and Emy had spent countless lunches, chatting about things that interested them both. At the next family meeting it was like seeing a different family. For the first time in years, they had begun to like each other.

Hugh's and Emy's marriage began to improve from that time on, and the quality of their relationship had a powerful, beneficial effect on their children. Although they hadn't seen the connection at first, their improved marriage was the necessary first step on the road to the eventual, effective succession and transfer of wealth. This is because the plans for transfer of wealth begin with basics, and the basics are the milestones of learning to communicate, to share, to raise the level of mutual trust, to develop teamwork and, finally, to express the affection and love that enables a group of individuals to become a real family.

If you're not communicating, sharing and expressing affection with your spouse on a daily basis, what you are doing is providing a negative role model for your children. A part of their growing up to become responsible, competent and healthy adults is to be given the experience of watching their Dad and Mom exhibit not only intelligence and competence, but affection, intimacy and love.

The reasons for remaining together are varied, and often include not only love for each other and concern for children, but comfort, convenience, mutual support, valuing shared experiences, and so on. After a period of intense and sincere communication, where partners take a close look at themselves and their lives, the marriage either gets better (if they both want it to) or it dissolves (if either one genuinely wants to dissolve it)—it rarely remains the same.

In the typical entrepreneurial family, Dad is usually off operating the business or managing family affairs and interacting with the world on a daily basis, while Mom has been charged with domestic responsibilities and, perhaps, civic or charitable work.

This makes for vastly different experiences which require very different skills. The effect of these different, daily experiences sometimes causes the entrepreneur to feel that he has outgrown his spouse, and there is no longer a basis for sharing. Conversely, Mom's exposure to a diversity of organizations and people may make her feel that her husband's interests have remained narrow, and so she, too, may feel there is no opportunity for sharing.

Different daily routines do not, of course, necessarily lead to incompatible partners. But busy entrepreneurs, whether male or female, often tend to avoid discussing their changing relationship with their spouse. Whether husband or wife, if one partner's values and interests change while their partner's remain static—and if there is no attempt to include the partner in the changes that are occurring—after a while there really is no basis for sharing. One-sided growth like this usually creates a lot of animosity and a difficult divorce.

Accepting your spouse and children for themselves is not always easy. Jordan and Margaret Paul give one reason why: "Have you ever wondered why grandparents are more loving with their grandchildren than they were with their own children? Have you noticed yourself being more accepting of other people's children than of you own? Nothing touches us as deeply as our family relationships. The more important the relationship, the more our fears and learned childhood reactions become activated. And we become unloving. We find it hardest to give love to those who need our love the most—our immediate family.",[1]

One of the effects of poor communication is that the love that does exist between family members is almost never expressed. If you, the entrepreneur, love your wife or husband and your children, but never say it aloud or by physical expression, they may not know it. In fact, studies have shown that if a husband and wife do not consistently touch each other at least 8-10 times per day, the marriage will likely deteriorate.[2] If you don't express your affection for them with hugging and other touching, as well as with kind words, they may not believe it even if you say it.

Among the families of our clients, we are finding more and more feelings of isolation, alienation and abandonment. So, if you really love your family, you have to find some ways to express that love to them other than just through gifts and providing material well-being.

It's often hard for a person who has been an entrepreneur for many years to express love. After all, love is giving of yourself unconditionally, with no strings attached and no judgments, loving that person whatever he or she is. What makes this hard for entrepreneurs is that so many of their business relationships are based on performance—I will admire and reward you based on how you perform in accordance with my standards.

We have a client—Noel Mandell—who is a rice grower...has about 2000 acres planted. Noel was estranged from his daughter for years. He wanted her to get an MBA and manage his agribusiness, but Catherine—he calls her Cat—got this idea to start her own printed circuit factory across the Mexican border near San Diego.

Noel hadn't seen her for three years and he was very unforgiving. He said to me, "Roy, she's doing it all wrong. I told her to get her education first but she just wouldn't listen." I told him that Cat was getting her PhD in the school of hard knocks, which for her may be a better way to learn. But Noel was stubborn; his daughter wasn't performing to his standards.

That year, when Christmas came, I said to him, "Why don't you go down and see Cat? That's what you really want to do, isn't it?" He admitted it was, so I said, "Why don't you get in an airplane and go?" Noel said, "I can't get reservations now; during Christmas, they're all booked." So I said, "So what? Charter a plane. It'll cost you a few bucks but you can afford it. Call up the airport, charter a plane and go down there.

Noel said, "Well, let me think about it." That usually means "no," but in this case, he actually did it. And he not only did it, he took his wife and his other daughter and her husband with him. They spent a week in Mexico with Cat. She was doing just fine. This was the first time he had ever gone somewhere without an agenda. One day he spent six hours reading in a hammock. It was the most restful vacation of his life. Most important of all, Noel realized that all his years of judging his daughter had kept him estranged from her—that the problem had been his.

When we talked about it after he came back, it became clear that Noel had had a lot of fear about love. He was a man who drove himself hard and rarely gave himself credit for his accomplishments. No matter how successful he was, he knocked holes in his self-image. And that was a big part of his problem. Because he couldn't accept himself, couldn't love himself, neither could he really accept or love others.

After a lot of soul-searching, Noel is finally learning that allowing himself to be vulnerable is not a weakness but a strength. Another way of putting it is that he's learning to cast out fears— fear of failure, fear of not measuring up, fear that others won't measure up. This has done wonders for his relationship with his daughter. Now he accepts her, accepts her decisions—he even asks her advice now and then, which is really something for Noel.

Love is an important element in our work with families and it is also important in my own personal life. I see it as the basis for everything we do and everything we hope to accomplish. I think it's really that way for everyone—at least that's my instinct. The problem is not so much the absense of love as much as the lack of communication of it. When people stop communicating, stop talking to each other with sincerity...or when talking becomes just a superficial exchange of words, that's when love seems to dry up. That's why, throughout this book, we will keep emphasizing the importance of communication.

Words aren't always necessary to communicate effectively. One way of giving and receiving love, without words, is through hugging. One afternoon I was interviewing Hal, the son of our clients Russell and Lonny Traborn. Hal is age thirty. At one point I asked, "Hal, how long has it been since your Dad hugged you?"

"I can't remember Dad ever hugging me. I don't think he ever has."

Then I asked Russ the same question: "How long has it been since you hugged your son?"

"Oh, I don't know...a few years ago, maybe."

"Well, Russ, your son says never, that you've never hugged him."

"That can't be, Roy. I must have hugged him...let's see...when he was ten."

"Why ten, Russ? Why not age fifteen or twenty-five? What makes you think of ten?"

"Well, when I was ten, my brother and I got a handshaking lesson from my Dad. I can still remember it lasted for about an hour. It included the proper look in the eyes, proper squeeze, all that. That was the only time my Father ever touched me. And I believe I did the same for Hal."

"Russ, are you open to hugging your son?"

"Well, I suppose so, but I want you to know, Roy, I come from a world where men don't hug men. My Father touched me that once. He loved me, but he wasn't a toucher, and neither am I."

"Didn't anyone in your family show affection?"

"Roy, when I was thirteen I was sent away to boarding school. They taught me to think in terms of math, science and English. What they never, ever teach you at boarding school is how to be intimate or vulnerable, because the moment you're vulnerable, someone's going to take advantage of you.

"Roy, I'd send letters home to my Mom and Dad, and get the letters back a week or so later, with corrections made to my English. Do you think I wanted to keep sending them letters?"

Russ choked up at that point, and I paused for a few moments until the strong feelings subsided. Then I continued. "I understand, Russ, but let me ask you this: will you hug your son?" "Yes I will, but...I need some help...in breaking the ice, if you know what I mean."

"I know what you mean."

Before the next family meeting I met again with Hal. "Will you go along with your Father hugging you?"

"It's not going to happen, Roy. My Dad will never hug me."

"But are you open to it if he does?"

"Yes, but I'll believe it when I see it."

At the family meeting we made considerable progress in sharing values. Everyone was feeling pretty good, and closer than they had been for some time. When I asked about expressing love, all family members admitted they wanted to be more affectionate with each other. The timing on this had to be just right, and this was the right time. I said, "Okay, what about a hug all around? I'll start," and I hugged a rather reluctant Russ and started on the others. Then Russ went around the room and hugged his daughters, and then, without too much hesitation, their husbands. Then it was time for his son, Hal.

Russ walked up to Hal and they stood there, looking at each other. Russ's arms reached out part way...he just couldn't do it all by himself. Hal said, "Oh, Dad," and wrapped his arms around his father. Then they were hugging each other tightly as if they would never let go. Both of them broke down and cried.

At that meeting they broke a longstanding taboo, a pattern that had existed in that family for four generations. After the meeting, Russ's wife, Lonny, came up to me and said, "Roy, I've been waiting my whole life for this...I never thought I'd see it."

The Traborns weren't bad people—not Russell, not his son, Hal, not even Russell's parents who had returned his letters, corrected, when he was a boy. They all loved each other but they didn't have the tools to allow them to get past their history and built-up habits.

After that first hug, Russ and his son began to do more things together. Since they were both interested in track and field sporting events, they went together to several track meets. They also rediscovered that they both liked chess. In fact, as with most families, the family members found out they all shared many values, and that same meeting was filled with "hmmm's" and "ah-hah's" from both the parents and their grown-up children as they were uncovered.

Of course, each individual family member is going to have some different ideas—and that's okay. But one of the real satisfactions that comes from family communication is to see that your children, and your grandchildren in their own time, have absorbed the basic values of life that you, yourself, hold in high regard.

With many entrepreneurs, a venerated value is respect for, and responsibility in dealing with, money. In an instance I'm thinking of, a client gave his grown-up daughter $35,000 because she was in debt and had no way to get out. With the $35,000 in cash, instead of paying off the debt, she put a down payment on a boat, thereby creating more debt. Her father was outraged, and screamed at her that she was stupid and irresponsible and could not be trusted with anything.

But let's examine the situation more closely. The daughter had had no training or experience whatsoever in dealing with money. On the contrary, she had been sheltered all of her life—all of her bills had been paid by others and, to a large degree, she had had access to unlimited funds. In addition, she had previously not fulfilled many of her promises about using money—and her parents knew it. So while her father knew she was sincere when she had needed the money, he also knew she was neither competent nor reliable. When he gave her the $35,000, he was really setting her up for failure. How much better off they both would have been if he had acknowledged that his daughter wasn't yet able to share his values about money, and he had given her some assistance in becoming more competent. In this way, they would both have grown from the experience.

When mutual values are understood and respected by family members, they're ready for the next step: developing family goals. Why are family goals needed? Drs. Jordan and Margaret Paul give a good reason in their book on parent-child relations: "An old Chinese proverb states: 'If we do not change our direction, we are likely to end up where we are headed.' The application for families is clear: parents need to take the time to reflect on goals for their families. No one would think of running a business without setting goals, but amazingly few parents take the time to do this for their families.", Gertrude Stein put it another way by defining insanity as when people continue to do the same things over and over but expect different results.

Family goals, of course, depend a lot on each individual's view of happiness and success. Is success to be measured in monetary terms, by degree of education, by the number of awards received or by how much good has been done for the world? Is happiness to be defined as lack of anxieties, as comfort, as self-acceptance or as joy and enthusiasm? A coach is of real help here, because the children of entrepreneurs often don't know what happiness and success are—money and objects have too frequently been the only measuring stick.

For several years this was a problem for the Hansen family. Leonard Hansen was a successful entrepreneur—he manufactured machine tools. He also had an admirable art collection. Len and his wife, Gail, got so wrapped up in their art collection that it seemed to take over their lives. Family happiness and success were determined by how many fine paintings they owned.

Between the business and the art collection, the Hansens had no time for their children, and nannies became the mentors. The parents were mostly absent on long trips, searching for additions to the collection. When they were home, there were endless social gatherings within the art world. Meanwhile, the kids were growing up strangers to their parents.

It took the Hansens a long time to realize that they'd gotten hooked by the possession of things and by status. Now, when the children are in their late teens and are getting ready to leave home, Dad and Mom have belatedly realized that their children are more important than their collection. It's still possible to overcome the years of neglect but it will be costly in terms of time, energy and persistence.

The issue is whether success is going to be measured by material possessions or by how family members feel about themselves. One of the initial objectives of the family getting together in periodic meetings is to see if all family members can find some common elements in their definitions of success and happiness. If your family can't agree on what constitutes success and happiness, it's difficult to develop many common goals.

There are some basic questions that have to be answered before family goals can emerge. For example, what is the family? Is it Mom and Dad and the kids? Does it include the spouses of the grown-up children? Does it include the grandchildren? How about step-brothers and step-sisters?

Another question that helps clarify family goals is: What do we mean by long term? The Iriquois Indians planned goals in terms of seven generations. People in some Asian cultures plan in terms of hundreds of years. In the U.S., it's a rare family that thinks and plans beyond the first generation.

In the next chapter, we'll look more closely at the meaning of happiness, success and fulfillment, and how your family can begin to identify goals through a system we call the Five Equities.

1   Paul, Jordan and Margaret, *If You Really Loved Me*, Compcare Publishers, Minneapolis, MN, 1987

2   See *UCLA Alumni Association News*, March-April, 1981

     Dresslar, F.B., "The Psychology of Touch," *American Journal of Psychology,* vol. 6, 1984, p. 316

3   Paul, Jordan and Margaret, *If You Really Loved Me*, Compcare
     Publishers, Minneapolis, MN, 1987

7 Feelings, Values and Goals

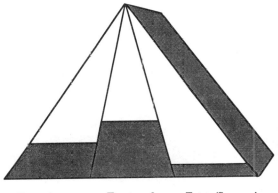

Preparing   Trust and   Estate/Succession
Heirs   Communication   Planning

A very close friend of mine shared with me an intimate story about feelings. When he was fifty-three years old, someone asked him "How do you feel about your family?" He replied that his son was doing pretty well, his daughter, recently graduated from college, was spinning her wheels and doing nothing and his wife was having a minor health problem.

His replies all concerned how he thought about family members. But the questioner wanted to know how he felt—if he was frustrated, sad, exhilarated, etc. As my friend pondered the question, he realized that he had never consciously acknowledged a feeling in his life. His newfound insight was the beginning of a magical transformation from brain to heart, and an awareness of a world he had long ago buried.

Feelings, although sometimes painful, are wonderfully true indicators of what's really going on inside of us, so awareness and acknowledgement of them are important. When we repress or ignore our feelings they can remain inside us as hidden manipulators, compelling us to action or inaction that is not in our interest and sometimes filling us with anguish.

It has been my experience that when we are divorced from our feelings, it's easy to go astray. I see that happening in many of our institutions. In our legal system, for example, lawyers and judges are fond of saying we are "a nation of laws and not of men." What this suggests, of course, is that laws protect us from the tyranny of unrighteous acts by others. Yet everyone who has been involved with legal matters knows that laws can be manipulated for unethical purposes.

I recently went to lunch with two partners of a well-known law firm, and we talked about the legal system. After some time, I asked this question: "Where does justice fit into the system?" They were silent for a moment, with incredulous looks on their faces. Then one of them said, "You're not really that naive, are you, Roy? What do you mean, justice? That term never enters into the conversation in this law firm. The only issue is to win or lose. And you had better win. Period!"

When the law becomes depersonalized, the victims are not only the litigants, but the principles of everyone involved. An acquaintance of mine illustrates this with the following true story.

"I was driving through the city of Oakland a few months ago, and I witnessed a terrible accident. An elderly woman drove through a red light in a busy intersection. She didn't notice a motorcycle crossing the intersection. I watched in horror as the motorcycle and rider rammed into the side of her car. The rider was thrown into the air and landed some twenty feet away on the pavement. He was wearing a helmet, but the impact was so severe he lay unmoving, his legs twisted into a grotesque position.

"After he had been carried into an ambulance and taken away, I and several other witnesses described the accident to the police. A few days later I made inquiries and found out that the young man had survived—barely—with a broken back and pelvis, multiple fractures of his legs and serious internal injuries. I learned that he was twenty three years old, married, with two toddlers. He had been an auto mechanic.

"I heard nothing more about the accident for two months, and I assumed that all claims were being settled without my being called as a witness. But one morning, an insurance investigator came to see me. He was representing the woman driver's insurance company. They had pressured her to declare that the motorcycle driver was at fault, and the investigator had come to see if he could get a witness to confirm her story so they could get a judgment against the young man.

"I asked him about the latest news of the young man's condition. He told me the medical report stated that he was permanently paralyzed and had undergone several operations. He would probably not be released from the hospital for another six months. I asked if the woman who was the cause of the accident had been to see him, or his wife. The investigator replied, "No, we strongly discourage any contact with opposing claimants." A few minutes later, he left—without my corroboration.

I was really bothered by his visit. I suppose there is some merit in keeping insurance claimants apart after an accident—after all, the injured party might try to murder the other one. But it seems to me the system shielded her from any responsibility for her actions. She didn't have to face what she had done—it was simply a legal matter, to be handled by legal experts.

"But what would have happened if that woman had seen firsthand the pain inflicted on the young man; if she had seen the face of his young wife at the hospital, day after day, for months; if she had seen the little children and realized that she had forever deprived them of a normal father—if she had seen any of that, and if she had any feelings, could she have allowed her insurance company to try to place the blame on him?"

Each of us has probably heard some variation on this theme. The principle is that we know, we feel, that we have a responsibility to our neighbor; but the law often says, no, we don't have a responsibility to our neighbor—we have a responsibility to follow our lawyer's advice. We don't go talk to the injured person and we don't apologize or try to make amends. We have been seduced into accepting a rational argument (let the lawyers handle it) in place of human decency.

An interesting example of moral vs. rational argument is in the experience of Anatoly Sharansky, the Russian dissident, who spoke of his years spent as a prisoner in a Soviet gulag.[1] The gulag officers and guards constantly tried to justify their own behavior and break the spirit of the prisoners by trying to convince them why their incarceration and harsh treatment were justified. They used all manner of arguments to do this: the prisoners were the parasites of society; all they wanted was disorder and chaos; they were scum who did not appreciate all the Soviet Union had done for them; and so on.

Sharansky's captors had all the advantages. In addition to weapons, they had good food, good health, warm clothing, news of the outside world and the ability to punish prisoners indiscriminately, which they did. Many of the inmates succumbed, and others, in order to get a scrap of food or a piece of clothing to avoid frostbite, admitted that they were indeed guilty and deserving of punishment.

Sharansky watched the KGB break the spirit of his fellow prisoners. When this happened, they began to weaken and die—their will to live had been broken. He felt his only strength, his only advantage was to cling to his moral sense of right and wrong. The KGB, with their gulags and tormentor guards, were wrong!

There was only one way to survive. Sharansky recounts: "I had to remind myself that the basic rule of the game is that moral principle is much stronger than any rational argument."

This is also true in our society. Your values are the bedrock of your morals and ethics. Although you may intellectually understand that following the Golden Rule is the proper way for you to live, in practice, it is your heart-felt values that ultimately guide you. When you see someone being wrongfully hurt, it is those underlying values that make you want to help, not your reasoning. This is what causes an otherwise unassuming person to spontaneously jump into a river to save a drowning child.

The Kronner family used to be an example of non-expression of values. I first mentioned the Kronners in Chapter 2, and how they never told their college-age children anything about family finances. In fact, there was not much communication in general between parents and children.

Phil and Jessie Kroner have been involved in charitable projects for many years, but their orientation has been on the amount of dollars spent each year on philanthropy. Their desire to give to charities, while heartfelt, has been expressed as an abstract principle; they haven't been involved with the actual people who were overseeing the projects or with those who were receiving the benefits. Consequently, their children have grown up to think of charitable work as a numbers game rather than issues affecting real people. But last year, Phil and Jessie funded a group that was working in the Sahel region of North Africa, where they're always having trouble with drought. And without telling anyone, their son, Kevin, who was studying mechanical engineering in college, designed and tested a new ultra-simple, bicycle-powered water pump for use in developing countries. It's a neat gadget—it requires only about $100 dollars worth of parts for the whole thing, plus the use of a local bicycle.

Kevin got together with his sister, Julie, and together they created a proposal to manufacture the parts and make kits available. When they presented their proposal to their parents, they did it with such enthusiasm that Mom and Dad got all excited, too, and wanted to fund the project and get it going immediately. The kids agreed, and, two months later, a contract was signed to make prototypes, develop an on-site test program and, within a year, manufacture the parts for several thousand units.

This was the first time that the Kronner family worked together on anything. One day, when the project was getting underway, Phil took his son and daughter aside and said to them, "I'm just so proud of both of you that I really don't know what to say." That was the first time the kids ever saw tears in their Dad's eyes. It was a whole new experience for all of them.

When it comes to helping family members to express values and feelings, one of the best tools of communication is the family meeting, which I described in Chapter 3. The rules that prevent emotional scarring and the presence of a skilled coach all work to make the family meeting a safe and effective way for family members to become familiar with each other's real feelings. The next step in the Integrated Wealth Transfer Process™ is to make the leap from feelings and values to goals.

After we have reached a certain age, perhaps as young adults, we all hold deeply-felt personal values. For convenience, we divide these values into five categories, which are:

- Physical Values
- Intellectual Values
- Psychological Values

- Financial Values
- Spiritual Values

Some Physical Values

What do you believe your body should be like? What should it be able to do? What is your ideal for good physical condition? Do your physical values include health, strength, vitality, agility, grace and beauty? How about the maintainance of good health when growing old?

Some Intellectual Values

Your intellectual values probably include the development of knowledge, experience and thinking skills. They may also include creativity, love of learning, using mind to its fullest extent and the gradual acquisition of wisdom.

Some Psychological Values

What are the most important things to you about character, personality and relationships? Some of your psychological values might have to do with integrity, self-acceptance, and maintaining one's principles. They might include the areas of friendship, caring and trustworthiness.

Some Financial Values

How important is wealth to you? What is the purpose of wealth? Are your financial values closely tied in to independence, freedom, power or luxury? Is the way in which you acquire money a part of your values?

Some Spiritual Values

Most human beings have an inherent need for spirituality—a built-in striving to seek meaning and purpose for their lives, and to have some kind of relationship with the Creator. This need assumes that there is some spiritual agency or force that is more good, more knowing and more powerful than ourselves. Your governing values for spiritual equity might include, for example, faith in God; the importance of love, compassion and good deeds; the search for meaning; and the purpose of your time on earth.

So we have established five categories of personal values. Now, why do we call our deeply-held personal beliefs values? Definitions of the word value include: the monetary worth of something; a fair return in goods, services or money for something exchanged; the relative worth, utility or importance of something; and so on. So we call our deeply-held beliefs values because they have value— they are worth something. In fact, our personal values are the bedrock, the foundation for all of our accomplishments in life. Everything we do is ultimately based upon our values.

So our deeply-held beliefs are valuable and, like other assets, they can be very beneficial if clearly understood and used effectively. Because they are assets, at The Williams Group we call our deeply-held beliefs equities, and the system of clarifying and using our personal values is called the Five Equities.[2]

Now our values give rise to goals. For example, if I believe that it is beneficial to have a healthy, energetic and attractive body, then this is one of my values. From holding this value, one of my goals, then, will be to arrive at and maintain my body in good physical condition. With that goal in mind, I can formulate the specific steps I will need to undertake in order to get there and stay there.

This may seem simplistic, but there are good reasons for going through this procedure. One is that we all occasionally need to look at our own lives to see if our goals really reflect our values. A second reason for looking closely at our own values is to see if we are on track and making progress towards our goals. Third, the process forces us to be specific in how we will reach our goals. And fourth, the sharing of governing values and goals among family members provides a comfortable setting for each family member to share important things that do not usually get expressed.

The Five Equities procedure connects personal values to goals, via daily activities. For example, in the Intellectual category, one of your governing values might be to use your intellect to its fullest possible extent. From this value, you might decide that one long-term goal might be to go back to school and earn a degree in the humanities. From that long-term goal, the Five Equities procedure formally helps you to spell out your intermediate goals. You might decide that over the next two years you will take certain courses that apply to the degree program; plus you might commit yourself to a diverse reading program where you read a minimum amount each day. The point is that to uphold your life values, you need to formulate long-term and intermediate goals, and to support these goals by the activities you do each day.

In this process, we encourage family members—especially the younger ones—to frequently review their daily activities to make sure that they are actually doing those activities that will lead to their longer-term goals. The Five Equities procedure provides a big boost in this area by keeping everyone on track. It provides a way of regular monitoring of our daily activities to ensure they are supporting our personal values. In this way, our personal values are not just abstract principles tucked away in the closet—we are actually living them.

There are two separate and distinct parts to the process of using the Five Equities. The first part is for the purpose of more clearly identifying and developing each family member's own values and goals. This is a private procedure, done alone by each person. The second part of the process is the sharing of personal values and goals with other members of the family. This latter part is never forced upon anyone, but it is an extremely powerful method that provides insight into individual values and needs.

The process of identifying your life values, deriving your short and long term goals from them, and progressing toward these goals by your daily activities is highly beneficial. It's a means of bringing your principles and your activities into productive balance. This may not be the first time you, the experienced entrepreneur, have thought about and identified your life values and goals, but it is highly probable that it hasn't been done by your children. For them, this exercise opens a whole new way of looking at their lives. It says to them, "How will you direct your life so that you can really live what you believe in? Will you plan it and be in charge, or will you allow yourself to drift on, reacting to events as they occur?"

The second part of the Five Equities process—the sharing of values and goals—is where dramatic changes frequently happen. For what may be the first time in their lives, Mom and Dad are hearing their kids talk about things that are very important to them, things they've never had the opportunity to express. And on the other side, the kids, by hearing about the values and goals of Mom and Dad, start to better understand why Dad is involved with the business and what it means to the family. This is powerful stuff. In a safe atmosphere, free of the fear of being attacked or ridiculed, all family members are baring their souls to each other.

In Russ Lackland's family, going through the Five Equities caused a real breakthrough. Russ's son, James, the oldest of three boys, was being groomed to become President of the family business, which is a land title company. Ever since James started college, it had been assumed by everyone in the family that he would be President—the subject was never even discussed. In fact, James didn't want to be President but he couldn't stand up to his strong-willed father and tell him so outright.

After all the Lacklands had completed their Five Equities sheets, we held a family meeting. I had met privately with individual family members prior to the meeting, and I was able to assure the children that it would be absolutely safe for them to express their innermost feelings. I had also told Russ that his son had something important to express to him, and that it was crucial that he allow the boy the space to say what he wanted. During the meeting, each person shared his or her values and goals with the rest of the family.

There are always surprises when family members share like this for the first time, and the Lacklands learned much about each other that they hadn't known. But when it was James' turn, and he quietly read off what he had put down on his sheet, there was dead silence in the room. It was immediately apparant that this young man had no interest in being President. In fact, he had no interest in business at all. The information from his Five Equities showed that he was strongly drawn to spiritual values. After sharing his values and goals, James looked at me for support, then turned to his father and said, "Dad, I want to go to a seminary and become a minister." It took Russ Lackland some time to come to grips with this, but he did. And in the process he started to pay more attention to his other sons, and how they might or might not fit into the business.

When you share your deepest feelings with others in an atmosphere of mutual respect, whether you've known them a short time or all your life, a new kind of bond is created. It's as though, for the first time, all of the masks we wear have been removed, and we see the real human being—unique, individual and precious. The sharing of their deepest feelings was a real turnaround for the Lacklands. Dad and Mom began to listen to their sons and to see that their opinions were valid. Their sons, in turn, realized that their parents weren't mechanical authority figures, but were real people, with real feelings and problems and needs.

Your values and goals, as well as those of your family, are not set in concrete; you'll change them as you, yourself, change. But regardless of how you change, the Five Equities process will help maintain a vital connection that enables you to live your personal values on a daily basis. I cannot recommend it highly enough.

This chapter has been about keeping in touch with our feelings and sharing them with our family. It is very important that we stay in touch with our deep feelings, for they are the basis of our values, and our values motivate our actions, whether we are aware of it or not.

Having a way to express feelings in a safe atmosphere is particularly important in keeping a family together. When family members express opinions about practical matters, these opinions may easily be criticized and/or ignored. But when family members express the deep feelings, the motivation which gives rise to their opinions, then their opinions are seen in a new light, and they command attention and respect. It is an axiom, based on our long experience working with familes, that the more family members are able to share their feelings, values and goals, the closer that family will be and the more certain the achievement of their goals.

1   "Sharansky In SF: Games Yes, But Not With The KGB," *San Francisco Examiner*, February 1, 1987

2   The Five Equities system, Alan Boal, Idea Transfer, Inc., San Clemente, California

8 When the Children are Young

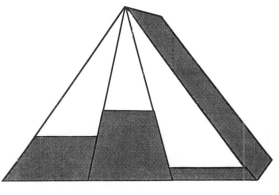

| Preparing Heirs | Trust and Communication | Estate/Succession Planning |

In Fortune Magazine, billionaire H. Ross Perot tells about the day, many years ago, when a reporter was interviewing him and his small son, Ross Jr., walked into his office. "So, young man," the reporter said, "how does it feel to be the son of the richest man in Texas?" "Mister," replied the boy, "all I know is I get twenty-five cents a week."[1]

It's an engaging thought, isn't it? A billionaire's son getting only 25¢ a week. Most people who hear this story feel good about it because it's demonstrating several sound principles. It tells us that the boy certainly wasn't being spoiled just because his family was rich, and that he was learning the discipline of money by receiving a regular, modest allowance. It also tells us that his parents were wise enough to begin his training at an early age.

This story about Ross Perot Jr. contrasts with stories of other families, where parental absence, neglect and inattention are more common. In one instance a man recalls of his childhood, "I kept hurting myself. I had these little accidents—crashes. I had this little scooter and I kept falling off it and riding it into barbed wire fences. I was always trying to do myself in (so that) I could get attention from my Mom. Mom came running down and picked me up...and was around serving me and helping me. It was great."[2]

Another man remembers from his childhood: "We were lonely. It was disappointing when my father would take off a lot for business. That definitely contributed to a lack of close relationships. One thing that was tough was my parents would go away for a vacation and leave us with a nurse. But, of course, she could never substitute for Mom and Dad. This became sort of an unwitting weapon that they would use against us, their going away. We were never physically beaten up but we always would feel that when they would go away they were punishing us somehow."[3]

Often, in the absence of parental attention, a nanny takes on the role of mentor to the children. One of the problems with this is that the nanny, although well intentioned, may have entirely different values than do the parents. Then, as the children grow up reflecting the values of their nanny, strong conflicts may arise between the values of the children and those of the parents. It's like rolling the dice—are you willing to take this kind of risk with your children?

In contrast to parental neglect when the children are young, some entrepreneurial dads, who are used to dominating their business, dominate their children as well. This is what happened with Porter Scudder and his only son, Miles. Porter had built up a good-sized commercial bank by a combination of skill and tenacity. He was single-minded and never let anything get in his way for long. He was also single-minded about raising his son. He wanted Miles to fill his shoes as President of the bank—there was to be no question about it. By the time Miles was five years old, his father had so dominated the little boy that he had lost all initiative. By the time the boy was a teenager, he had lost any natural decision-making ability he might have had.

The terrible irony of this is that Porter, by so rigidly raising his son, had produced a man who was totally incapable of being President. When Porter died, Miles, because of his stock holdings, took over as President. He was an abject failure. After one year, the board moved him to the position of Chairman, but with no decision-making powers. Today, Miles is an unhappy, frustrated man who would be much happier working as a clerk or cashier, with limited responsibilities.

The learning of initiative, responsibility and accountability needs to start early in childhood. When children don't develop these qualities, it often turns out that these missed experiences have negative results later on. When parents fail to follow through on things like allowances, or solving school problems, they lose vital opportunities to build their children's character. By the time the parents realize that some character flaws are present, the children may be older and already out of their grasp—spending most of their time at school, playing sports and out with friends.

As Drs. Jordan and Margaret Paul put it, "Giving teenagers responsibility for their lives when they've been tightly controlled is frightening. The decisions they have to make are much more serious than those that have to be made at six or ten years old. Kids who have practice with decisions don't have so much trouble. When young children have a chance to practice making decisions, they are better equipped to make the more important decisions as they get older."[4]

Many coddled children are missing some fundamental values because they never had to work for anything while they were growing up. They weren't allowed to have a newspaper delivery route because mom worried about their safety; they were discouraged from baby-sitting because Mom and Dad were too busy to chauffeur them around. By the time they were teenagers, they hadn't learned anything about job responsibility or how to handle money.

This is what happened with another client of ours, Hal Moreland, who had built up an international commercial real estate business. Hal, himself, was the soul of integrity. He did business on his handshake, and his word was his bond. He gave value for value received, usually throwing in "a little extra" because he believed it would ultimately be more profitable than driving hard bargains. Hal personally trained all his staff to work with a creative, noncompetitive attitude. By the time he retired at age seventy, Hal Moreland's name had become synonymous with integrity in international real estate circles.

Unfortunately, Hal had devoted so much of his time to building the business that he had neglected his own two sons, Owen and Cass. He had left their training to his wife, who was also away from home much of the time. After she died, as they were finishing high school, the boys were left pretty much on their own. When Hal sent Owen to the Wharton School in Philadelphia, and Cass to the Harvard Business School, he told himself that he had fulfilled his parental responsibilities. Owen and Cass took over the business when Hal retired, a few years later.

We came into the picture about ten years after the sons had taken over the business. They had mismanaged it terribly; their questionable tactics had nearly run the business into the ground.

Their Father had built the business based on people, trust and integrity. Owen and Cass, in contrast, tried to keep it going on the basis of opportunism and tight margins. Their motto was, "Make a deal, shop around, re-deal or get out." They used slow pay to make money on the float. They interpreted the casebook lessons they had learned at Wharton and Harvard to mean, "Screw the other guy before he can screw you." Their Dad, who was a model of integrity, is probably turning over in his grave at their behavior. But it was caused, at least in part, by the fact that he had never gotten around to teaching them his values.

Teaching children self-reliance and accountability is a good way to start. Taking the training wheels off is always a judgment call, as any parent knows who is familiar with skinned knees and elbows. Money accountability helps children develop good, personal values at an early age. The mistakes they make in their savings accounts, what they save money for and what they spend money on, are all small things. But as they grow up, these experiences will help them to manage bigger things and will also give an indication of their character.

Children, like adults, learn from mistakes. But it is also vitally important that lessons in self-reliance and accountability result in some measure of success for your children. If their experiences commonly result in failure, their self-esteem will be sorely damaged and they will come to view self-reliance and accountability as negatives.

From my experience with clients and their families, I've come to see just how crucial a positive self-image can be. Self-image is largely built up from early childhood experiences, which set in place patterns that can repeat throughout a lifetime. Even in the face of later, positive experiences, these behavior patterns tend to remain dominant and unchanging. Unfortunately, with many families, and especially families of wealth, children's negative self-images seem to be built into the family system: the dominating Father has unrealistic expectations from his children and, when one of them doesn't meet his high standards, he yells something like, "What's the matter with you, dummy, can't you do anything right?" Mom typically reacts to this by trying to protect the child, but this only provides a path of temporary sanctuary for the child, it doesn't improve the child's self-image.

A few pages back I described how a banker, Porter Scudder, had so dominated his son that the young man was totally ineffective as President of the bank. A more extreme case is that of Don Jessup, who owned a farm equipment company. Don expected his only son, John, to grow up as he, himself had: tough and hard-hitting. When the boy failed to do this, he bore the brunt of his father's verbal abuse. Internally, he crumbled at the constant negative judgments, absorbing early and often the message that he was incompetent (and thus unlovable). Don's wife, Marilyn, in an attempt to neutralize her husband's influence on the boy, added to the tragedy by trying to raise little John gently. This only increased the Father's abuse of his "sissy" son.

This boy never had a chance. His self-image is rooted in the belief that he is ineffective and a nonperson. His values are all oriented to avoiding pain and surviving. He has never learned how to be an independent human being and, according to him, the greatest thing that has ever happened to him is the tremendous relief he felt when his Father died.

Many times, the busy entrepreneur Father or Mother doesn't spend time with the children and tries to buy their love with money and gifts. But, when the only reward or expression of love and support the children receive is material possessions and/or money, then possessions and money become the measure by which the children judge their self-worth. If, for example, a son perceives that he has received less from parents than they have given to another sibling, then that son will not only be resentful, his self-esteem will also be diminished.

Working with many families over the years, we have seen that competence is the forerunner of self-esteem. The more competence young people (or anyone else, for that matter) develop, the higher their self-esteem. So how do we help our children to become more competent? At The Williams Group we begin by introducing families to seven different levels of competence beginning with the lowest and ending with the highest.₅

1) Bull in a china shop

2) Pretender

3) Beginner

4) Minimally Competent

5) Proficient

6) Virtuoso

7) Master

No. 1: Bull In a China Shop

This person doesn't understand that he is having an influence in a given area; he is blind to his own incompetence and the negative effect of his actions.

No. 2: Pretender

This person is aware that he can't perform competently in a given area, but does so anyway. He causes suffering for himself and others, and even though some part of him knows he is incompetent, he may live in partial or total denial of his incompetence.

No. 3: Beginner

This person is aware of his lack of competence in a given area. He admits that he is a beginner, declares that he is willing to learn and finds, and gives authority to, a coach.

No. 4: Minimally Competent

This person performs to commonly accepted standards and needs occasional supervision. He does not look ahead and therefore cannot see potential problems or the need for change.

No. 5: Proficient

This person's competence usually exceeds accepted standards, without supervision. He solves current problems adequately, anticipates future problems and is able to plan for required changes within his area.

No. 6: Virtuoso

This person consistently performs above acceptable standards with ease and grace. He anticipates near- and long-term problems and is able to innovate skillfully within a given area. His skill in this area is acknowledged by others.

No. 7: Master

In addition to performing as a Virtuoso, this person is capable of inventing entirely new fields of activity (examples: Einstein and relativity, Edison and electricity).

We begin the process of developing self-esteem by encouraging family members to evaluate their own levels of competence in areas that are relevant to that family. Once, during a meeting of my own family, my son, Scott, who was sixteen at the time, was asked what he wanted to do with his life. He replied, "I don't know what I want to do, and I'm scared to death because I don't know."

Scott was acknowledging he was a Beginner. As a result, he immediately gained the support of other family members and of the advisers attending the meeting, and he learned that it was okay if he didn't know something—as long as he was willing to learn.

Levels of competence cover many areas. For example, it may be important for the children to attain a high level of competence in running the family business . But what about money management or family philanthropy? And how about their people skills? Are they able to help the family work together as a team or are they at the lowest level of competence—a Bull In a China Shop— causing family problems without even being aware of it?

Evaluating levels of competence isn't limited to the children. Dad may acknowledge, for example, that he's been so involved with the business that he's never really learned how to be a father—or grandfather. Acknowledging that he's a Beginner in this area opens the way for him to develop more competence.

After we go through the process of having family members acknowledge their competence levels in areas of importance to themselves and to the family, we help them develop their own road maps for increasing their competence. Once they have evaluated their current levels of competence, these road maps detail the steps required that will take them to the higher level of competence desired.

Not everyone needs to be a Virtuoso or Master in every area. In the family business, it may be that a son or daughter needs to learn to become merely Proficient in, let's say, the research, production and shipping departments, before moving on to management.

The impact of this system of evaluating levels of current competence, and establishing desirable future levels, is very powerful. We go into familes where the heirs don't know what they don't know. Young MBA's, for example, may be taking actions even though they do not comprehend the results of those actions.

Later, when levels of competence have been sorted out, the family is able to avoid unpleasant—sometimes catastrophic—consequences. In addition, the former image of failure carried by one or more family members is replaced with one of candid acknowledgement, and determination to learn and do better.

As I said earlier, self-esteem is based upon competence. We can't give our children self-esteem. The best we can do is to create the circumstances that will help them to develop their own competence, which will enhance their self-esteem.

It is particularly important for Dad, the successful entrepreneur, to avoid setting standards for children that are based on his expectations. Dad assumes and expects that everyone else in the world, including his own children, has been blessed with his initiative. Yet motivation and initiative are things that cannot be taught.

Helping build self-esteem in your children is quite similar to building self-esteem in your employees—you provide them with challenges that will stretch their abilities but not exceed them so much that you are inviting failure. Children thrive on positive reinforcement and praise (who doesn't?). Be sure to take the time to praise your children's accomplishments whenever and wherever you can. That doesn't mean that there should be no accountability—you need to let them know when they have done poorly. But it is crucial that your criticism is constructive and encouraging. Instead of the "You dummy!" style, be sure it comes out something like, "Yes, it's hard, but I know that you're smart enough (or strong enough or brave enough) to do better, and it's important that you try just as hard as you can."

Helping to build self-esteem in children is a long process that requires attention, insight and sensitivity day after day, for years.

For the children of affluent parents, there is an extra burden in the building of self-esteem. That burden is the denial of wealth. In family after family, we have found that the children think poorly of themselves, and of how others view them, because their family is affluent. Many of them buy their clothing in thrift stores to try to counteract their embarrassment over family wealth. It's a situation where the children rarely talk about it with their parents, but are constantly aware of it.

I know young adults who have run off to Central America to live in poverty, while they leave all of their money with trustees...sometimes for many years, until they get through the denial stage. One young woman wanted desperately to be treated just like her peers, but her friends found out that her family went on vacations to a private island off the Florida coast and that her family owned part of the island. That changed something in the way her friends viewed her; to them she had suddenly become different, separate, and she hated it. This woman now shuns any outward signs of wealth. She dresses plainly, never makes any but modest purchases and never, never talks about her family with others. She rarely gives her address or other information about where she lives to her friends. Until she felt safe enough to speak about this during one of our family meetings, this woman had never mentioned any of this to her family. She's been living a lie, denying her affluent status, and it's been very painful for her.

On the surface, denial of wealth is caused by not wanting to seem different from friends. But additional probing frequently reveals biases not only against accumulated wealth, but also against business and profit in general.

Ironically, the daughter of one of our clients was totally unaware that her father, a successful businessman, was one of the most beloved persons in the community, and consistently gave much of his own time and energy as well as his money for worthy causes. One conversation I had with the daughter, Diane, went like this:

"I think 'profit' is an ugly word. I don't want to have anything to do with the business."

"Wait a minute, Diane, do you think your father is an honest man?"

"Yes, I think so."

"How about integrity? Does he have integrity?"

"Yes."

"Do you think he uses money wisely? Do you know how much he does to help others?"

"Sort of, but I know he keeps a lot of it."

"Diane, have you ever heard the story of the pitcher? If you are an empty pitcher, every relationship you have is to get somebody to put something into you; but if you are a full pitcher, then you can give and give and give because you've got something to give. Have you ever thought of it that way?

"No, I guess not."

From that, the conversation went into the nature of the family business, how many people it employed, and the good that its services did. It turned out that Diane was totally ignorant of what her Dad was doing—in business and in the community—she had shunned knowing because of her discomfort with wealth.

Until this young woman can start to address this issue from a healthy standpoint, she may be emotionally crippled and may never be able to be a responsible, accountable person who can inherit wealth and have it be an asset rather than a liability.

Slowly, we are trying to encourage responsible young adults not to be embarrassed by growing up with money. We have tried to help these young people to understand that money gives them options, and among these options are opportunities to do some wonderful things for Humankind.

They don't have to be embarrassed, they don't have to denigrate the family business and business in general; what they need to do is learn to be creative and help figure out the best uses for their money.

Shunning wealth is similar to shunning power. Many children of our client families know that their fathers or mothers are "powerful," but that power seems to them to be a negative thing. TV shows all repeat a similar theme: powerful people take advantage of weak people; they misuse their power.

In contrast, when a daughter talks, for example, of "empowering women," power is seen as a positive force. So it isn't that power, of itself, is bad or good; power is neutral, and can be used for bad or good. It can improve lives; it can even save lives. When we work with families, we define six kinds of power.[6]

1) Military

2) Financial

3) Personal

4) Intellectual

5) Productive

6) Institutional

If the military destroys a town or, through its airlift capacity, averts a famine, that's military power. If the boss tells an employee, "Do this or you're fired," that's financial power. But if a minister, without financial power, is able to persuade his congregation to make donations for a new church school, that's also power—personal power. If a science teacher delivers a stimulating lecture and many students are inspired to take up science careers, that's intellectual power at work. If a Henry Ford designs an affordable car that changes the way society operates, that's productive power. And lastly, if local government officials build a dam that floods a valley and forever alters the area, that's institutional power.

Power is the ability to generate action, to effect change. We show the children of our clients that power is always created by an observer. If someone is all alone, they don't have power; it is all of us observers that allow power to be used. And, sometimes, we allow power to be misused. For example, when a famous singer or actress gets involved in politics and uses her personal power to endorse a candidate, she is straying into the area of institutional power—an area of power which we observers haven't given to her. And her image, and career, may suffer as a result. Or take the example of doctors. We give surgeons the power of life and death over us...an immense power based on their training, which is an intellectual power. But in terms of financial savvy, the surgeon may be a disaster. Ignorant of investment procedures, the surgeon assumes, incorrectly, that because he is powerful in one area, he will automatically be powerful in another.

What we are saying, here, is that when someone attempts to use their base of power to wield another kind of power beyond their area, they may temporarily succeed, but in the end they will lose power, not only in the new area but in their original area as well.

Now all of this talk about power is not merely a theoretical exercise—it has very practical applications. For example, if your children inherit money, that doesn't necessarily empower them. If they grow up untrustworthy so that no one wants to deal with them, what power do they have to generate effective action? So, we need to help them develop their personal power in order to make good use of their financial power.

By understanding the nature of power, and the different kinds of power, we are opening up new vistas for the children of our clients. As a result, they no longer have a knee-jerk, negative reaction to power. They now see it as a potential force for good.

∞○∞○∞○∞○∞○∞○∞○∞○∞○∞○∞○∞○∞○∞○∞○∞○∞○

When we first meet the children of clients, we often encounter prejudices against wealth and power, as I've discussed here. In addition, many of these children dislike—even abhor—what their fathers or mothers are doing. They don't understand why they feel this way and the parents don't understand either. I've covered many of the reasons in the previous chapters: lack of communication among family members; children not understanding the business; the children seeing many of the negative influences of the business on the family, such as the time Dad spends away from home; or cash-flow crunches where the business gets all the available money while the family may have unmet needs.

Typically, Dad doesn't come roaring home and announce to the whole family that he's gotten a new contract, or that his team has just come up with a new product and that it's tested perfectly; Dad comes home late, tired, sometimes irritated at all he's had to put up with that day. The kids see all this negative drain and stress on the family without ever seeing the positive side of what the business provides—the strokes Dad gets, and the financial reward. The subliminal message says, "Baby, if you go into business, you'd better be tough and you'd better be willing to pay a high price."

They get the message and say to themselves, "This is not what I'm going to do. There has got to be an easier way to live than what my Dad goes through."

Like most problems in life, a grown-up son's or daughter's aversion to the family business often comes from ignorance. The best way to have your kids become more interested in the business is to get them involved. I recently spent some time with a family where I made the comment to the father that he is going to have to spend time with his daughters—spend time educating them on the nuances of how to buy and sell real estate, because that is his business. How do you go about finding a piece of property? Once you think it's a good piece of property, how do you buy it right? What are all the processes you have to go through to be able to build on it? What are the risks involved? He said to me, "Roy, that took me years and years to learn." I replied, "Isn't that exciting? Do you realize that it will take you years to teach everything to your daughters? Do you realize what a great avenue you've got for spending more time with them?" He had never looked at it that way, but he knew, instinctively, that it was true.

Some of my clients are farmers. Their sons have ridden in their pickup truck every day and have helped operate every piece of equipment from the time they were two years old. Some of those children want to be farmers as much as they want to eat or breathe. And they want to be just like Dad. In the same family, there are children who love Dad just as much but want nothing to do with the family farm. One youngster wants to be a concert pianist; another wants to be a merchant seaman. All of these dreams are okay. A passion is a passion.

How can you help your children or your grandchildren find their passion? As every successful businessman knows, running a business is one of the most exciting and challenging things you can do. If your kids pick this up, it will probably be because you've spent a lot of time with them, and the challenge, the excitement and the rewards will have rubbed off on them, plus the realization of what a fantastic opportunity they've been given.

Whatever their final choice, spend time with them on it. If your child really wants to try to become a concert pianist, take the time to check out piano teachers and schools, and go to recitals. Don't delegate it to someone else—stay involved! And remember, it's never too late.

The title of this chapter is, "When the Children Are Young." That has real meaning for me because I have come to see how important early training is. When I say, "early training," I'm talking about education in the broadest sense—the informal education that comes from watching Dad or Mom, or from being with another mentor. Informal education includes learning people skills: how to communicate well and to deal with people's needs and desires and complaints and idiosyncracies. Informal education includes the ability to weigh many factors and to make sound judgment calls, based on solid values.

In addition to informal education from parents, a formal mentoring program—in addition to formal schooling—is very desirable. There is a difference between a parent and a mentor. After about fifteen years old, kids no longer need parents as much as they need a mentor, someone who can teach them without the emotional baggage of parenthood.

How do you find and select a mentor? As you recall, we define the levels of competence and allow our clients' children to arrive at the understanding that they are Beginners, and that they need mentors. Then the search for a mentor begins. We can't select mentors for a family—they have to do it for themselves—but we can help point the way.

Mentors aren't going to be mentoring in a narrow specialty. They won't be teaching the youngster brain surgery or house construction. Rather, they will be teaching the broad skills of responsibility, dependability, integrity, using common sense, compassion, iniative, innovation vs. respect for tradition, risk assessment and so on.

Ideally, a mentor should be twenty to twenty-five years older than the Beginner. He or she may be a friend of the family, a relative, or a business associate of Dad's, or an acquaintance in another industry. The mentor should be someone who has been through the same experiences the young man or woman will be going through, and who can show the way. If one of the children's mentors is a nanny, it is terribly important to choose a nanny whose values and character you respect; a nanny should be chosen with the same care you would choose a company President—and perhaps be given the same respect.

A good mentor can't be bought. Mentors volunteer out of friendship and respect for the family, and the belief that they can be of real help. The young person must ask the potential mentor for help. He or she should go to work for that person...without pay if necessary.

There is a story about Aristotle that goes like this: A young man asked Aristotle to be his mentor. Aristotle replied, "Meet me at the ocean tomorrow." When the young man arrived, Aristotle took his arm and guided him into the water until they were almost submerged. Then, Aristotle suddenly gripped the young man in a head hold and forced him under the water. The young man, taken by surprise, struggled furiously but Aristotle held his head beneath the water. Moments later, the young man passed out, and Aristotle immediately lifted him up and carried him to shore where he revived him.

When the young man could speak, he said, "You almost killed me. Why did you do that?"

Aristotle replied, "When you want wisdom as badly as you wanted air when you were struggling in the water, then you will have it."

While the story is dramatic in the extreme, it makes the point that the Beginner must want to learn. He or she must also be able to ask for help. And this brings up another point: where it was once natural to ask for and receive help from our neighbors and friends, now we live more or less isolated lives, and we have become dependent upon government for assistance. Most of us have forgotten how to ask for help. So the very act of asking someone to be a mentor helps to establish the habit of asking for help when it is needed—a habit that will prove to be highly beneficial over a lifetime.

∞∞∞∞∞∞∞∞∞∞∞∞∞∞∞∞∞∞∞∞∞∞∞∞∞∞∞∞

I believe that children should get acquainted, at an early age, with how business works, what real estate is all about, and why there are stock markets. Children should be able to sit in on board meetings—business boards and charitable boards—and to learn the role of a director and of the board members. As soon as possible, your children should be included in social functions where they can interact with your friends and can be exposed to diverse topics of discussion.

In primitive societies, the children learn by watching their parents interact in all kinds of situations. When the family trades camels for goats, the kids get to see how it is done, and they gradually become competent traders themselves. One of the drawbacks of our modern society is that our kids are isolated from business transactions, and they don't get to see how Dad or Mom works, and to learn from it. With your children and grandchildren, try to get them involved and let them see how you operate. After they've watched you negotiate some issue, discuss it with them and tell them, on a level they can understand, what options you had and why you made the decisions you did.

It's very important, in the formative years, to expose your children to sound values, to sound judgments, and then to help them find a mentor and to allow them to gain experience in the real world. As a parent, you have the opportunity to be your children's most influential teacher—don't let the early years slip away without leaving your mark.

1   *Fortune Magazine*, September 10, 1990

2,3   Bronfman, Joanie, Doctoral thesis, "The Experience Of Inherited Wealth: A Social Psychological Perspective," UMI Dissertation Service, Ann Arbor, MI

4   Paul, Jordan and Margaret, *If You Really Loved Me*, CompCare Publishers, Minneapolis, 1987

5   Categories developed by Business Design Associates, Emeryville, CA

6   Developed by the Newfield Group, San Francisco

9 Developing the Family Team

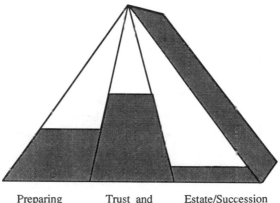

| Preparing
Heirs | Trust and
Communication | Estate/Succession
Planning |

Just as your business requires a strategic plan for its continuing growth, so does the goal of preparing your children to inherit your wealth. What is a strategic plan? It can be a comprehensive plan to educate your children across a wide spectrum of life challenges, or it can have a narrower focus. The example of Willis Dryden describes a plan for teaching his grown-up children money management. Willis owns a construction company and has one married daughter. She and her husband are both employed. Willis doesn't want his money to be a destructive influence in their lives. If they were to suddenly receive a large inheritance, Willis was afraid that the money might be a disincentive for them to work, and that it might be disruptive to them and to his grandchildren whom he loves dearly.

We interviewed his daughter, her husband and their children, to determine their attitudes toward money. Where, together, they're now making $65,000 per year, what would they do if they suddenly started receiving $10,000 more, $50,000 more or $100,000 more? These were not easy questions to answer, but we have made a start. The plan calls for Willis to form a partnership in which his daughter and son-in-law are partners in investment programs. Willis owns the investments and his daughter and son-in-law receive income from them in accordance with their degree of management participation. The idea is that the youngsters won't suddenly be confronted with substantial sums; over a 20-year period, they will gradually be introduced to more money as they learn how to manage it effectively.

This kind of plan requires a commitment from Willis to spend the time educating his daughter and son-in-law. So far, he has done well, and they have increased their annual income by $25,000 and are investing it wisely.

This kind of sound, strategic planning and implementing is still relatively rare. Too often the father will say, "I don't need help with a plan—I'll do it myself." Two years later, when I inquire about how his plan is working, I typically get a reply of, "What plan?"

Lack of planning for family time together is also prevalent. In many instances, Dad works himself to exhaustion and completes a big project. Then he suddenly comes home and announces, "I need to get away. We're leaving next week." This may be the only way they ever go on vacation. Mom then has to make all kinds of changes in her calendar (including the complications of what to do about school-age children). The sudden announcement deprives Mom of control and causes ill will between the couple. It's hard for the wife to coerce her husband into doing vacation planning because she doesn't know the cash flow situation of the business and how much money is available for trips. Nor does she know when her husband's work load will allow him to take time off. From his side, Dad resists vacation planning because he is so bound up in his business priorities. And while he is quite capable of planning business conferences and major capital purchases a year in advance, he cannot seem to give family activities the same high priority—they occur "when there is time."

One of the recommendations we make to our clients' families is that they set up a family calendar and create a family fun fund. In Chapter 6, I described how the children of Hugh and Emy McDowell planned an entire vacation by themselves, and how successful it was. Based on that experience, Hugh set up a continuing family fun fund, separate from the business, which each year generates enough income for a great family vacation, plus other outings.

Each November, the family members plan their fun calendar for the next year. Hugh can structure his time away from the business because he knows well in advance the dates to which he is committed. Emy knows how much income the fund will generate each year and she is in charge of the fun budget. Like Hugh, she can now schedule her own time and commitments, and she can make convenient arrangements for the children to take time off.

Hugh, Emy and the children decide, together, what constitutes "fun." While the fun fund was at first used exclusively for going on family trips together, as the children have matured and the amount in the fund has increased, "fun" now includes hands-on involvement with charitable causes.

The family time together has been a wonderful experience for the McDowells. For the first time since his wife and children can remember, Dad is putting aside time just to be with them. Hugh's wife, Emy, is delighted with the new arrangement. The planned, regular vacations have kept Hugh healthier and more vigorous. And Emy feels that she has more control in family affairs and a real voice in decision-making. The whole family is operating more as a team.

What happens with the many clients who have established family fun funds is that Dad has started to take family activities as seriously as he does the business. Family fun activities are planned the way any business activity is planned so that, in November, Dad knows what his commitments are for the following year. Family activities no longer get "bumped" from the calendar by business or other personal affairs. So far, with the aid of this system, none of our clients have gone back on their family commitments.

The idea for a family calendar started years ago, when I realized I needed to spend more time with my own family. I got together at home with my wife, Diana, and our children, and showed them my year-at-a-glance business calendar. At that time I was doing a lot of public speaking around the country, and some of my lecture commitments were a year or more in advance. Each November, I blocked out my time commitments on that calendar.

So I said, "Here are my current commitments. What dates do you want?"

I have three sons, and their schedules were complicated by the fact that each one went to a different school. Eric told me he wanted me to come to his football games. Danny and Scott wanted me to come to their basketball games. So we had to figure out how to plan my time with the boys, and our vacations and other family activities, and still accommodate all of my business commitments. I also told my sons that if I committed myself to time with them, it was necessary that I spend some time away from home, earning money, and I wanted their full support in this.

We made up a year-long family calendar that year and each subsequent year the boys were living at home. After that commitment, I don't think I ever missed a football or basketball game, and we all had marvelous times together. I didn't make as much money as I might otherwise have, but my relationship with each of my sons is very, very good. We have a similar arrangement now with our grandchildren.

If you don't include family activities in your schedule and you are deeply involved in running your business, it's very difficult to find enough time for family activities. Even when you do manage it, you are squeezing either the business or your family and it is a stressful situation. Creating a family activities calendar provides a useful structure to elevate and maintain family priorities. It has become one of the standard tools we recommend for all of our clients.

While part of the task of developing a family team is to raise the priority level of activities you share with your children, part of the task is learning to allow the children more independence at the same time. After I had made up a calendar for my own family, and had been faithfully attending my youngest son, Danny's, basketball games, he telephoned me from college one day: "Dad, I'm broke. I need some money."

"That's wonderful," I told him.

"What do you mean, 'That's wonderful?'" he replied, obviously puzzled.

"Because you're going to learn what it means to be broke," I said. "Isn't that exciting?"

"But Dad," Danny said, "I only need $200."

I remained firm. "It doesn't make any difference if it's $200 or $200,000. It's the same thing that you need to learn. I know you'll come up with the money somehow, or decide that you really don't need it all that badly. In the process, you'll learn how to avoid going broke again."

It was a hard thing for me to do. It's easy to love with money...to just give it to them...but it's a lot harder to love by denying them and risking their feelings for you. In this case, it turned out to be worth it. Three years later, when my son and I were talking together, he said, "When you wouldn't send me that $200, I hated you, just hated you." I asked him what he had done about the money at that time. "Well, I had spent my monthly allotment on junk and then I discovered I needed to buy some books for a lab. So I went to the student loan office and got a loan and paid it off over the next three months. I guess you were right about my learning, because I haven't been broke since then."

Danny had found his own way out of his troubles, growing in the process. With Danny, my instinct had proved correct. But deciding whether to give in to your children's needs or refuse them, in hope of teaching them a lesson, is sometimes a difficult judgment call.

In the case of Josh Park, a client of mine in New England, his son and daughter-in-law and their two small children were in trouble. They had just barely made their latest mortgage payment, and they were out of food. Josh and his wife invited them all over for dinner to discuss the problem. Here is Josh's version of what happened:

"We went over their present finances, how they got there, and what they could do about it. We didn't rescue them with money, though it would have been so easy. Instead, we restrained ourselves and talked with them about how they could raise some short-term cash. My son, Joel, was in real estate and he had two deals going that wouldn't close for another sixty days. I advised him that he might get a bank loan based on his accounts receivable, if his boss verified that the deals were sound. Also, he could refinance their house or sell one of their two cars.

"As it turned out, the bank wouldn't loan them any money. Joel did manage to close one of his real estate deals, and that gave them enough to exist for a few weeks. Then they sold one car, whittled down the utility bills, and cut nonessentials. This was a totally new experience for them—they'd never had to tighten their belts like that before. I thought they had done a good job at getting in the black.

"I'd been through belt-tightening experiences, myself, and it was not a big deal for me. But I guess I misread how strongly the situation had affected them because a month later we discovered that Joel had a bleeding ulcer. That's when I felt that I had made a wrong decision. Loving your son by teaching him a lesson is one thing—hurting him is another. I did a lot of soul-searching after that, trying to figure out if my principles were really valid or if I was trying to remake Joel in my own image.

"Two or three months later, Joel's wife, Nicole, confided to me that it had been a very difficult situation for them, but that the crisis really drew them together as a family. Joel's ulcer faded after a few more months, and all their bills got paid up—by them. I feel that I did the right thing, but I still have some guilt about it."

It's tough. Young people need to have their training wheels removed so they can try balancing on their own. They need to face mistakes and failure, and to know what it's like to pick themselves up and push on again. They need to build their own strong, self-confident images, preferably laced with a little humility. And they need to learn to be responsible and accountable—to themselves and to others.

When your children are in need, whether or not you decide to financially assist them is not the most important element in dealing with the issue; the most important element is how much you are personally involved. When you take a personal interest in their problems (if invited to do so), it shows them you care. Nothing else— nothing—can take the place of your personal involvement.

One of the mistakes successful entrepreneurs may make as parents is to treat their children with kid gloves, sparing them the rigors of responsibility and accountability. The case of Norm Schroeder illustrates my point. Norm grew up in extreme hardship, where his family was hard-pressed to feed all the children. Norm was self-taught all the way, and it was a hard climb to success. Today, he is a manufacturer of turbine components in Portland, Oregon, and his international sales are over 50 million. Norm's son, Jack, came to work for him a few years ago and Norm bent over backwards to give his son every opportunity that he, himself, had been denied. Unfortunately, that included treating him differently from the other employees. Jack soon learned that, as the boss's son, he could get away with just about anything.

When Norm hired a new Production Manager, Jack quickly let it be known that his privileged position meant that he wasn't to be ordered around. The manager knew that he had to run the plant or leave it. Without hesitating, he faced Jack and told him, "If you don't do what I've told you to do within the next 30 minutes, you're no longer going to be employed here." He then immediately reported the incident to Norm.

Norm backed the manager one hundred per cent. He called his son in and did something he should have done years earlier. He said: "I hired the new manager to do a job and his job is to run the plant. If you ever challenge his authority again, I have told him he can fire you on the spot. As for you, I'm sorry that I haven't said this before now, but maybe it's not too late. From now on you're on your own here. No more hanging on my shirttails and acting like the boss's son. I happen to think you're smart enough and competent enough to make it on your own. If you don't agree and if you don't think you're good enough to compete on that basis, you should leave."

This was a real shock to Jack—he'd never heard anything like that before. To give him credit, he stopped testing to see how much he could get away with and he started acting like a member of the team. It was a real turning point in his life. That was six years ago. He's now Vice President for Research and he's doing a great job— he's helped the company successfully obtain dozens of new patents that are proving to be very lucrative.

After teaching children responsibility and accountability, one of the next steps is allowing them to test their values and to take risks. Ironically, although entrepreneurs have had to become expert risk-takers themselves, they often fail to teach their children these skills. As parents (and grandparents), this is difficult to do because it goes against their protective instincts. But like it or not, children are constantly exposed to risks—in school, in sports and in relationships. And often their failures do more for them than their successes.

Sometimes, youngsters take risks that are inherently unwise, and they need to learn how to assess risks before they undertake something. When they have taken a reasonable risk and have failed, it's important to help them examine the effort that went into it. For example, what else could they have done? What did they miss? Was it mental or physical effort that was lacking, was it a deficiency in spirit or was it something beyond their control? Are they willing to put more effort into it the next time? In other words, are they willing to overcome obstacles in order to gain rewards?

Value-testing and risk-taking are necessary maturing processes—when young adults don't have opportunities to test the values they have received from their parents and to take risks and assess the results, their development suffers. Previously, I mentioned the case of Tom Wilbanks, who gave his daughter, Lynn, $10,000 to invest "as she pleased," but filled the air with dire pronouncements about the instability of the stock market, the hidden pitfalls in real estate, etc. Lynn placed the $10,000 in CD's and was never able to accept any degree of risk. All her adolescent years, her father had been giving her a mixed message: take risks but don't take risks. She chose the latter.

Children have to fail in order to learn what success means. They have to lie and suffer the consequences in order to really appreciate integrity. And they have to learn to rely on others and become part of a team in order to accomplish a goal.

Several of these points are illustrated in a classic story by Mark Twain called, The Man Who Corrupted Hadleyburg. In the story, the town of Hadleyburg has the reputation of having the highest morals in the region—and all the residents of Hadleyburg agree. One day a stranger comes to town with a sack of gold, and leaves instructions that it be given to an unnamed individual in town who had done a good deed in the past. The stranger doesn't say what the good deed was or who did it. As a consequence, everyone in town scrambles for the gold by claiming to be the one who had done a good deed worthy of the reward. In fact, the stranger's purpose is to debunk the high moral tone of the townsfolk by showing what happens when they are tempted by greed.

Twain's point was that we don't really know morality until we've been sorely tempted in the opposite direction. Similarly, with our children and grandchildren, we can't just teach them values—

we have to let them experience life for themselves. Some children grow up and spend their entire adults lives with their training wheels still on. This is compounded by the naturally-increasing conservatism of the mature entrepreneur. As entrepreneurs get older, they'll start to hedge their bets. The older they get, the more they want to put aside. The conflict comes about when the mature entrepreneur has an entrepreneurial, grown-up son or daughter who is ready to take some risks, but Dad says, "You risk your money—I'm not risking mine anymore." Then Dad has to find a way to teach the principles of reasonable risk-taking, using either his child's money or with a limited sum of his own.

It's an unfortunate irony when Dad, who made his fortune by thoughtful risk-taking, is unable to help his own children to do the same.

It is worth repeating that whether you decide to financially assist your children or not, the most important element in dealing with them is not how much money you give them, it's how much you are personally involved. Nothing can take the place of you demonstrating you care by taking a personal interest in their lives.

10 The Use of Money

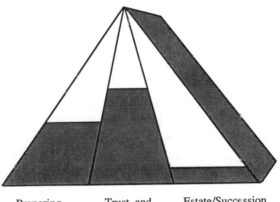

Preparing   Trust and   Estate/Succession
Heirs   Communication   Planning

We are making progress in our climb up the pyramid. Back in Chapter 8 we looked at the terms business, profit, wealth and power, and stated that although some children who grow up in families of wealth start out thinking of these as negative, we can demonstrate their immense potential for good. In this chapter we will do the same for the word that means so much to so many: money.

Janet Kolski is the entrepreneur of her family. She had seen money destroy too many families, and she felt strongly that she didn't want it to be a destructive influence in the lives of her own children. When they were teenagers, she informed her son and daughter that her entire estate, aside from the expense of their college education, would be going to charity—they would receive nothing.

During college, they worked at part-time jobs to have some extra spending money. After graduating, both the son and the daughter found jobs and were responsible for themselves, never receiving a penny from Mom or Dad. They were making modest salaries, earning their own way.

When we became involved as coaches for Janet's family, one of the things we discussed was the use of money. We used the analogy of a tape recorder and asked whether the electricity that powers the recorder is good or bad. Everyone understood, of course, that the electricity is a neutral force for tape recording. If we record lies in order to harm someone, then we are using that force negatively. But if we record an inspiring or informative selection that really helps someone, then we are using the force positively. Similarly, money is a neutral force that can be used either for bad or good.

In family meetings, Janet, her husband, her children and members of The Williams Group continued to discuss the idea of money as a neutral, but potentially positive tool. After some time, Janet came to realize that giving money or not giving money to her children wasn't the real issue—helping or harming her children was the issue. And with the tools the family was beginning to use: value clarification, family meetings, starting family partnerships, investment education and so on, Janet saw that her son and her daughter were developing enough maturity that she could trust their ability to handle money.

Janet changed her will and trust documents to reflect her new confidence in her children. And since she has done so, an interesting change has come about in both the daughter and the son. With substantial assets now under their control, they are beginning to act with considerable confidence and responsibility toward everything they deal with. I believe it is at least partly because they know their Mom is now saying, "I trust you with money."

Where her son and daughter were each earning about $20,000 a year, they are now sharing a much higher income. They have continued working in their jobs and are reinvesting that new income wisely. And Mom, in turn, has seen that money can be a positive influence in the life of young adults.

Janet Kolski is typical of many of our clients in that she is very balanced with money matters. She knows how to save and she also knows how to spend for good purposes. With others, that isn't always the case. The lack of balanced judgment often shows up in small matters. For example, after a meeting with a family in Indianapolis, the youngsters wanted to go out to the nearby fast food restaurant for a snack. I couldn't believe what the father said then: "Let's drink our drinks here, we've got lots of soft drinks here." "Why?" I asked, "Don't you like drinks with your hamburgers?" "Yes," he said, "but they make all their profits on the drinks." This was from a man worth millions. The message he was sending to his children was that no one was entitled to make profits except him.

When stinginess has to do with petty things, it's merely annoying to be around. But when real human needs are at stake, monetary mean-spiritedness is more tragic. We worked with one particular ex-client for several years—I'll call him George. During the last year we worked with him, in addition to counseling his family, we were able to pass on some ideas to George that enabled him to make an extra half million dollars.

That summer, I volunteered to do some fund-raising for a very effective local camp for underprivileged boys and girls. I had committed to raising money to send six children to camp for the summer—at $1500 per child. I had put in my own $1500 and I wanted to find five others to pledge the amount for one youngster each. When I put it to George, he asked: "Who's doing this?" I told him the names of the people involved and how effective the camp had been in helping poor kids get a valuable experience. Then George asked, "How much profit do they make on each kid?" I said, "I don't know...the cost is in line with what other camps charge. They're doing a great job for these kids. I've seen these kids after camp, and it's really impressive."

Although George had spent many years aggressively pursuing profits himself, and had substantial wealth, he declined to participate because he was afraid someone else might be making a profit.

In our experience, this is a rare exception to the rule, which is that most possessors of wealth are not obsessed with money— what they are obsessed with is accepting challenges and solving problems in order to make something work, and creating something of value. It's the challenge and the opportunities that inspires them, not the love of money.

In our society, children are not taught a philosophy of money.

As parents, we need to make a conscious effort to teach our children that money is not good or bad by itself—it's something that will give them options. With money, they can have a choice of what to eat or drink, while impoverished people must take anything they can get. With money, children have the option of working, enrolling in an inexpensive junior college or going to a top-ranked university—without money, their choices are more limited.

Our children need to understand that having money does not make someone a good or a bad person. There are good people who are rich and there are bad people who are rich, just as there are good and bad people who are poor.

Money can be used in ways that give it a life of its own so that its benefits multiply throughout society. When we meet with clients' children, we get them to think about the positive aspects of wealth. Here is a list of positive uses of wealth drawn up by the children of one family:

- To live comfortably and provide for family needs
- To allow independence and freedom for family members
- To provide a reserve in case of an accident or sickness in the family
- To improve community at all levels from local to international
- To fund and improve sports, the arts and charitable programs
- To create businesses which provide jobs for people
- To help the poor

We then ask them to list some negative aspects of wealth:

- Controlling others
- Buying your way out of problems you've caused
- Causing envy by your having more money than others
- Buying too many material things just because you can do it
- Using money as a substitute for caring and spending time

with people

From there we go on to ask: "How much family money should go for philanthropy and how much should stay in the family? What criteria should be used to determine who gets the money? What are the rules for giving away money?" And so on.

One way to introduce philanthropy to our children is to include some philanthropic element in trusts. When the trust directly involves them in some kind of charitable endeavor, it makes the abstract concept of philanthropy come alive. The philanthropic element also helps to assuage guilt they may be carrying when they inherit wealth, and it justifies their inheritance. Some of the grown-up children of our clients have gone a long way toward solving their problems with wealth by adopting an active philanthropic focus, giving not only their money, but their time and energy as well.

Establishing a family foundation is an effective teaching tool for your children. It encourages them to think. What should be the purpose of a family foundation? When we meet with families, we answer this by working with the entire family, including the children, to develop a mission statement. Next we help family members determine if the family lawyer has the skills to correctly form a foundation. If not, we provide the criteria and help the adult children to select a lawyer for the family foundation. This gives the children added competence in hiring, and it forces them to learn how to present complex matters to the other family members. As this inter-family communication unfolds, issues of trust, reliability, competence, honesty, etc. will come up and be dealt with.

While many corporations and affluent families contribute generously to charitable organizations, often there is very little involvement or follow-up to determine whether or not the money is being used effectively. Where family members have some responsibility for family philanthropy, it's important that they have a real feeling for the causes they want to help. The first thing we do together is to use Abraham Maslow's "Hierarchy Of Needs", as a guide (Starting with practical needs such as food and shelter, Maslow's Heirarchy lists successively loftier needs, ending with spiritual and aesthetic needs.) This helps family members decide, for example, if they are more interested in organizations that pro-

vide food and shelter, health services, tackle environmental problems or support the arts, etc.

When we have identified the causes that family members feel
strongly about, we ask them to research the organizations that
address those needs. A part of this research involves finding out
how efficient a particular charitable organization is—that is, what
percentage of its income actually goes toward its stated purpose
and what percentage is used for administrative costs and fund-
raising. Some organizations actually spend a majority of their income on fund-raising. This is usually a real eye-opener, especially
to the sons and daughters. Each charitable organization has this
information available to potential donors. It is also available for
most major charities from certain periodicals and private organizations.[2]

We ask the sons and daughters to personally check out the
organizations of their choice to see if they like working with the
staff members, and to get as much first-hand information as they
can about the work the organization is accomplishing. When family members have decided, together, what organizations they want
to support, we next introduce a time/money guideline. Dad and
Mom, together with any advisers that are needed, determine how
much money will be available for charitable causes. Then we ask
the sons and daughters what amount of total time they are willing
to devote to charitable causes and, of that total time, how much
time they will give to each organization. The time/money guideline requires that they can only give money to an organization in
proportion to the amount of time they are willing to work with
that organization. For example, assume that $100,000/year is avail-
able for donations, and all sons and daughters, together, commit
themselves to giving 20 hours of their time per month. If they want
to give half of that money to a particular charity, they must spend
at least half of their time, or 10 hours, working directly with that
charity.

This forces them to know what is going on with the charity of
their choice, and how their money is being used. Parents love this
system because it imposes discipline and responsibility on their
children and because the involvement is a real education for them.

I have a client and close friend, Bob Graham, who is an exemplary role model for the good use of money. In his travels in the

1970's, Bob developed an acute awareness of the disparity and resources between the U.S. and the Third World. Vowing to do what he could to help, Bob decided he would implement a "50/50 at 50" plan—when he turned fifty years old, he would devote half his time and resources to service and half to business.

In 1985, Bob founded a non-profit international development organization called Katalysis. Working closely with indigenous, self-help groups in Belize, Honduras and the Caribbean, Katalysis has helped thousands of poor farmers and small business owners, disadvantaged women and unemployed youths gain the skills and resources to become self-reliant.

Bob, his wife, and his six children are all active in philanthropic work. The family meets twice a year to review their "social investments." In addition to teaching his children about using money, Bob also engages his children in projects that make money. The family's joint involvement with philanthropy and money management has been a challenging process that has taken considerable time and effort to work out, but it has brought the family much closer together.

Bob Graham is a man who knows that money can be used for much more than just making more money. Through his socially-responsible projects, he has not only helped countless others but has enriched his own life and the lives of his children as well.

While wealth does confer responsibility, it also provides unique opportunities. Some wonderful things can happen through the creative use of wealth: profound benefits for society, and immense education, satisfaction and fulfillment to the families who have learned to work together to make it happen.

1   Maslow, Abraham, "A Theory Of Human Motivation," *Psychological Review*, Volume 50 (1943).

2   An extensive ranking of charities is given in the December 14, 1995 issue of *The Christian Science Monitor*.

The Better Business Bureau publishes a listing of national

charities through its Philanthropic Advisory Service, 4200 Wilson Blvd, Arlington, VA 22203.

The "Wise Giving Guide" is available from the National Charities Information Bureau, Inc, 19 Union Square West, 6th Floor, New York, NY 10003.

A listing of evangelical charities is available from The Evangelical Council For Financial Accountability, PO Box 17456, Washington, DC 20041.

11 Involving Your Family With Money

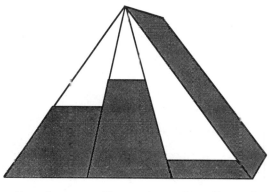

| Preparing Heirs | Trust and Communication | Estate/Succession Planning |

The ability to manage money isn't inherited, it is a skill that has to be learned. John D. Rockefeller Jr. certainly believed that, for he raised his children in an atmosphere of stern monetary discipline, even though they were surrounded by servants and luxury. Each child had to keep an account book of his weekly allowance, extra earnings and expenditures. The allowances were so low that the children had to do extra work around the house in order to have any pocket money. In our own families, we may not elect to have such strict discipline with our children, but we certainly should not leave the development of their money skills to chance.

With young children, school vacations are good times to give them experience in handling money, when they are less busy with homework and school-related activities. One idea that works well is to let them pay all household bills during a summer. This lets the children learn the value of electricity and water supplies, the costs of automobile, food, clothing, medical and other purchases. At an early age (perhaps 13-14, depending on maturity), I suggest that you arrange for your children to get checking accounts and credit cards, with limits on them. We usually recommend beginning with $25 to $50 limits. Together with this privilege is the requirement that each week, or month, they must show you a balanced checkbook and a fully-paid-up credit card. We also suggest that you offer to match any amounts your children earn, from allowances and extra jobs, that they are able to save over a period of time.$_1$ Children have to learn how to make money, how to keep it, how to spend it and how to deal with debt. The checking account, credit card and the ability to earn more by saving (from your matching funds) empower your children, and though they will make mistakes, they'll learn from them and will become more responsible and accountable. Also, this kind of parent-child cooperation will help you to enhance good family communication on a topic with which you are at ease and well-versed.

From the time your children are small to when they become young adults, the more time you can spend with them sharing your business and financial knowledge, the more prepared they will be to handle money. After they have completed college and are working and/or parenting, even if they have received an MBA, we recommend that you send each of your children to one of the small business programs available at several universities or at OMBI.$_2$ They teach a broad range of practical business issues that aren't found in academic programs. These small business courses aren't cheap, but they will educate your children to the point where you and they can talk the same language when it comes to the family business and finances.

In families of affluence, one of the things that taints the possession of wealth for the children is the secrecy with which the subject is surrounded. Many children grow up with the feeling that the family money must be bad because its specific value must be hidden and never discussed openly. In addition, the children get the message that they cannot be trusted with this information. By avoiding the subject, the childhood attitude that something is wrong about having money may persist into adulthood. Of course, for the grownup children, there are also societal pressures of not wanting to seem ostentatious, and fearing that if friends know their family is wealthy, the friendships will be threatened. But the negative, early childhood feelings about money seem to persist in many cases.

Here are a few comments from grown-up children about hiding their family's wealth:

"If my roommates or somebody went out and bought a dress or some shoes and boots, they would come home and parade it. I would bring it home in a brown bag and run it up to my room and hope nobody had seen it, and hide it, and then a few days later when I would wear it and somebody would comment on it, I would say, 'Oh no, I've had this for years.'"[3]

"I was trying very hard to hide and it meant that I couldn't talk about anything related to my background. After a while...I felt that there was nothing I could share, that there was nothing it was okay to talk about."[4]

"I was always terrified they were going to find out somehow, and very often they did. I think I came across as being a very retentive, unsharing person who kept much, a whole lot, to himself."[5]

In early family discussions having to do with family assets, Mom and Dad usually talk in generalities. They'll ask us to present general information to the family on the subjects of estate taxes, charitable gifts, and so on, but not about specific numbers. There is a valid reason for this. For example, when a child is five years old and asks, "Where did I come from?" there are a variety of possible answers. In one case, the mother gave a detailed reply about the human reproductive system. When she had finished, her little boy commented, "Mom, I didn't want to know all that, I just wanted to know if we're from Cincinnati, like my friend Tommy."

The young child isn't prepared to understand all the details. It's a similar situation with specific questions about money; children, even grownup children, have to be prepared for dealing with specific figures. Even though family finances are discussed in generalities, it is important that the subject be treated openly because *young children already know when their family is affluent.* This comes from simple impressions, like the fact that their home is bigger than those of their friends, it has more telephones and other appliances, and so on. Denying wealth simply creates mistrust of parents.

If the topic of specific numbers is off limits, it is important to state this openly to the children—that this subject is not going to be discussed for a while. It is a legitimate position and, because it is treated openly and directly, the children will probably accept that. The problems occur when, instead of simply stating their position, the parents hedge and waffle on the subject. Then the children feel that their parents are hiding something, with all the ensuing attitudes that are picked up and carried to adulthood.

As the children grow up and become more knowledgeable about money management, *and are mature enough to handle it,* Dad and Mom should divulge more information on a step-by-step basis. Parents have a tendency to withold this information even after the children are ready for it. At the same time, this is a highly personal decision for the parents—they have to feel comfortable talking about specific numbers with their children.

When discussing specific amounts of money, parents must be prepared to back up their policies with answers. At a family meeting, one young child asked, "If the family earns $200,000 per year, why do we only get $1 per week?" Or a young adult might ask, "If we each will be receiving a $100,000 inheritance, why do we have to wait when *now* is when we need money the most?"

Also, parents need to feel that their children are capable of keeping specific information within the family and not telling others. In working with families, we suggest that knowing certain details of family wealth is helpful to the children, while divulging other details may be harmful to the family.

Money skills are fundamental to acquiring or maintaining wealth. Much strife among families is caused by the fact that many children—even the grown-up children—are lacking in basic money skills. They certainly don't know how to produce money—only how to consume it. They don't know how to balance a check book or understand how or when to borrow money, and certainly don't know how to invest it. They don't know how to use their skills effectively to exchange them for money.

When parents give money to their children, they are watching to see if the children use it wisely, and whether or not they are able to use it to learn how to produce and not just consume.

We begin addressing these problems by applying observable and measurable standards to the two basic area of personal finance, which are *money skills* and *wealth skills.*[6] The reason for standards is to let them see where they are so they can begin to look at what they need to do in order to improve. In the areas of money and wealth skills, we help them judge their own competence in accordance with the levels of competence I presented in Chapter 8, which are:

1) Bull in a china shop

2) Pretender

3) Beginner

4) Minimally Competent

5) Proficient

6) Virtuoso

7) Master

Money skills have to do with producing and consuming— making money and spending it. Most youngsters, of course, are better at spending it than making it. A person who is incompetent in this area will not be able to manage cash flow, and there is a continuing imbalance between producing and consuming. For individuals who acknowledge they are beginners and are willing to learn, we assist them in understanding the basics of personal finance, help them establish standard practices for managing cash flow, and bring them up to a minimum standard of managing cash flow. After a one year period, we assess their abilities to confirm that they are independently competent in the area of money skills.

Wealth skills have to do with borrowing and investing. Many of the children of our clients don't have an understanding of the nature of borrowing and investing. We demonstrate that when we invest, we are taking an action in the present in order to gain a result in the future. It is an exchange. Something is sacrificed now in exchange for some gain in the future. Borrowing is, of course, the opposite. We receive something now, and in return we promise to make a sacrifice in the future.

Incompetent persons in the area of wealth skills will borrow more than they can manage and frequently get into trouble trying to pay it back. They will have little or no understanding of investing. For individuals who acknowledge that they are beginners, we assist them in learning borrowing and investing fundamentals, establishing investment management practices, and we bring them up to a minimum standard of managing their investment portfolios. After a one year period we assess their abilities to confirm that they are independently competent in the area of wealth skills.

With our clients, we have found that one of the best ways to begin to involve children with family assets is to set up informal family investment partnerships. These can start when the children are in their high school or college years, or when they have left home and are married. Whatever age the children are, the dollar numbers have to be large enough to get their attention. As an example, let's look at the partnership we helped set up for Leonard and Gail Hansen and their two sons and two daughters, ages 19 to 28.

In this case, the initial funding was $150,000. If the partnership investments yield a 10% return, 15,000 will be earned the first year; if the yield is 15%, the income will be $22,500. That makes the sons and daughters sit up and pay attention. This is no longer some abstract discussion about succession which will impact them twenty-five years later—it is real income that is happening now.

The Hansens decided to initially share the income from the partnership on a basis of 70% to Dad and Mom and 30% to be divided among their children. While Leonard and his wife, Gail, provide the capital, the sons and daughters actively participate. As the young men and women learn more about investing and their participation becomes more valuable, the percentage of income they receive will increase. The income that the sons and daughters earn from this partnership is theirs to do with as they wish. Will they consume it or reinvest it? How they handle this income gives Dad and Mom a good opportunity to judge their current attitudes about money.

Another of our objectives for this partnership is to have good family communication about investing. With our financial coaches assisting, the family discusses questions such as: What are our investment objectives? What are we going to invest in this year? What level of risk are we willing to accept?

This is a great way to get grown-up children involved and educated and to learn to work as a team. Though the rewards begin the first year, we encourage both parents and their children to view the investment partnership as a long-term effort stretching ahead for fifteen to twenty years. The long-term goal for the Hansen family is that by working together each year, even though their children marry and create their own families, all of the family members will gradually begin to think of themselves as a coordinated team where all participants benefit.

There are different ways of structuring a partnership. In my own family, I formed a different kind of partnership with my three sons. One of my main goals was for my wife and my sons to learn about partnerships. In this partnership, my wife and I were 1% owners and general partners, and my sons (and myself also) were limited partners. As general partners, my wife and I controlled the assets, but the partnership agreement gave the first 10% of all income to the limited partners. So my sons had a strong interest in making the partnership profitable.

This partnership owned a building, and we had to decide who was going to manage it. As it turned out, my wife became manager and, since she didn't have any background in managing buildings, there was much for her to learn. Our sons had to confer regularly with her in order to make the operation work, so it was also a good way to stimulate communication.

While partnerships that include all family members are very helpful in promoting family teamwork, separate partnerships between Dad and each sibling or Mom and each sibling are also useful. For example, if one of your sons becomes interested in buying a building, parent and son can establish a separate partnership devoted to that purpose without having to involve the whole family. This allows the young person room to learn and take risks on his own.

Sometimes there are legal requirements which limit the activities of an existing partnership, so that if new activities are to be pursued, new partnerships have to be established. Separate partnerships between parents and their children also teach how unrelated partners can work together where, for example, one partner has the capital but no time or interest in active participation, and the other partner has no capital but has energy and motivation to get things done. This type of partnership also permits a close, one-on-one relationship between Dad or Mom and each sibling.

Legal partnerships between a parent and one son or daughter

can also include a buy/sell agreement which indicates how either partner can dissolve the partnership and get out. This provides the basis for determining each partner's capital and/or energy contribution, and how much each partner will receive from partnership assets.

While legal partnerships between parents and their children are good teaching tools, they require a strong commitment from parents because of the necessary paperwork, including filing partnership tax returns. They also require that the entrepreneur-parent, who has probably functioned as an independent decision-maker in the past, now has to coordinate with his sons and daughters to make partnership decisions. This became a critical issue with one of our clients, Elmo Budd, and his two sons in their late 20's. Elmo wanted to involve his sons in a partnership venture, a start-up brewery, that looked like a good deal. He said he was going to commit $500,000 to it. Though the sons were both college graduates, they had had no experience with partnerships, and they waited for some word from their father about what to do next. They waited for several months and finally asked their mother, who was more approachable, what had happened to the brewery deal. Mom told them that Dad had decided it wasn't a good deal after all, and had dropped the plan.

True to his old habits, Dad hadn't discussed anything with them even though they were supposed to be partners. At a family meeting, this subject was raised and the sons said to me, "We don't want to be partners with Dad because being partners means we have nothing to say and no voice in the decisions." We then discussed with them how a real partner can't move without the consent of the other partners, and they responded with, "Well, our partner didn't act in good faith." This was terribly embarrassing for Elmo, who was seated not ten feet away. He knew they were right and he felt badly that he hadn't followed through on consulting with his sons.

Many good things came out of this. His sons not only learned what a partnership was supposed to be, they learned that they could challenge a partner even if it was their father. For his part, Elmo learned the importance of keeping an agreement with his sons. This is a particularly crucial point. I cannot emphasize enough the importance of parents keeping their promises to their children;

if Mom or Dad sees some reason for canceling or modifying a promise, it should not be done unilaterally.

There was another important thing Elmo had to learn from this experience. He was forced to move out of an entrepreneurial role, out of the father role, to a peer-level where he was a team player.

Elmo did finally explain to his sons why the brewery was a bad investment, and their communication began to improve. Ultimately, they found better investments and their subsequent partnerships have been successful.

The effects of a partnership on family relationships and on the children are impressive. When the partnership is working as it should, it is a powerful educational tool. Imagine the confidence that comes when one or more of the sons and daughters, together with Dad, have bought a piece of property, created a joint-venture, or learned about managing a building or a shopping center. Imagine the effect when a son or daughter can say, "I earned $20,000 and paid my own taxes on it. Now I can pay for my own education—Dad doesn't have to give me the money." What a sense of pride and accomplishment and independence! And Dad is no longer viewed as a hard-nosed businessman who doles out pittances; now he's a trusted partner whose value to the partnership—and thus to the children—is obvious.

∞∞∞∞∞∞∞∞∞∞∞∞∞∞∞∞∞∞∞∞

While the family entrepreneur has had a lot of experience managing a business, he or she probably is not nearly as experienced in managing passive income; that is, income which comes from assets outside the business and over which the entrepreneur has no management control. Let me give you an example. One client of ours, Gregg Pergem, sold his company and ended up with eighty million dollars after taxes. Because he didn't know what else to do with the money he put much of it in CD's at $100,000 each—hundreds of them! He had banks calling him every day, and he had stacks of bank messages on his desk, asking, "Should we roll this over? What are your instructions?" He was very frustrated. This was a man who was a business school graduate and a very sharp businessman, but he simply had no experience handling passive income, and he was overwhelmed by the magnitude of the cash.

Here's another example. As reported in the Wall Street Journal,[7] the investment firm, Capital Insight Brokerage of Beverly Hills, lost up to $100 million from corporate and private portfolios. Among the corporate accounts were Pier 1 Imports, Inc. of Fort Worth, Texas and PairGain Technologies, Inc. of Tustin, California. When they were asked "...why such longstanding corporate clients, and dozens of well-heeled individual investors from around the country, failed to heed repeated warning signs about (Capital Insight's) high-risk investment strategy, a number of customers acknowledged that they regularly received but failed to analyze or ask questions about daily and monthly summaries of futures and options trades made on their behalf." The CEO of PairGain Technologies, Inc. was quoted as saying, "I get statements, I look at them, file them and don't understand them."

The above story is not an aberration—this kind of thing happens all too often. So it's fair to ask: Why do so many entrepreneurs, who have been highly successful at building and running a business, do so poorly when it comes to managing money? For one thing, it requires a lot of time and energy to learn how to become competent in managing money, and most entrepreneurs feel they are too busy to commit time to it. So it's ironic that these highly successful entrepreneurs, who are on top of every facet of their business, avoid doing the due diligence necessary to manage money properly.

One of the things our coaches[8] do is help the family determine what information is available and what isn't. We ask these kinds of questions: What is it costing you to have someone or some organization managing your investments? What is your overall rate of return on investment, after all costs are considered? How has your overall rate of return compared to average market performance over the same period of time? What is your current net worth?

When we first began working with families, decades ago, the results were surprising. No longer. Most heads of families did not know the answers to these questions. And when they finally probed deeply enough to find them, the answers often were that their costs of investment management were far higher than they had thought; their overall rate of return on investment was lower than they had been led to believe and, in many cases, it was lower than market average; and their current net worth was less than they had anticipated.

Once we have gained the necessary, fundamental information on the family's portfolio, we introduce two differing investment concepts: Performance-Based investing and Wealth Preservation.[9] Performance-Based investing is the traditional one with which we're all familiar: the greatest investment rewards go to the smartest investors. To do well, you must either be a smart investor, yourself, or you must hire a smart investor to beat the market for you.

Where appropriate, we help the family to agree on risk limits. For example, is the family willing to invest partly in high-growth, speculative issues or do they want to invest conservatively, where the maximum return will probably be less than 10%, with a very low risk of loss.

As a part of this process, our coaches help family members agree on some subjective investment criteria. For example, are family members opposed to defense contractors who manufacture weapons systems? Are they opposed to investments in foreign countries with poor human rights records? Do they favor certain investments such as companies breaking new ground in conservation, medicine or education?

When the Wealth Preservation process is selected as the favored investment process, the family, together with our coaches, begins by defining an investment and consumption policy consistent with preservation and long-term growth of wealth. The family does not try to beat markets that have been proven difficult to beat. They stop paying high commissions, management fees and unnecessary taxes, and stop taking the unnecessary risk that goes along with trying to beat the market. Instead, they establish policy guidelines for investing in low cost, broadly diversified portfolios of domestic and international stocks and bonds, and for periodically rebalancing to meet asset allocation targets while minimizing capital gains taxes.

Whether a family chooses to follow traditional, Performance-Based investing or the Wealth Preservation concept, a clear picture is still needed of how their investments have performed, the cost of investing, their total net worth, etc. We emphasize top-down monitoring of the following:

- What are current return-on-investment expectations, based on predictions?

- What are the current asset allocation targets, based on computer modeling?

- What is the current asset allocation position?

- What is the expected return for the current position?

- What expenses are associated with maintaining the current portfolio position?

- What is the current net worth?

- Is the family consumption plan in balance with a conservative view of expected return?

- Are managers operating within their policy guidelines?

- How have investments performed relative to appropriate benchmarks?

- What is the overall rate of return of the portfolio?

One of the most important aspects of our financial coaching is that the children are actively involved in the process. By their involvement, they are approaching the question of money management from a rational and methodical standpoint, and they feel empowered because they are encouraged to help make investment choices. The parents, too, are learning, and they can see their children are learning a process that will serve them well in the future.

By involving the everyone in the investment process, once again the family has taken a giant step forward in preparing the children to inherit wealth and to manage it wisely.

1   *Teaching Your Children Responsibility, Teaching Your Children Values, Teaching Your Children Joy*, Linda & Richard Eyre, Simon & Shuster, New York, 1994

2   The Family Business Program, Owner Managed Business In-

stitute (OMBI), Santa Barbara, CA

3,4,5 Bronfman, Joanie, Doctoral thesis, "The Experience Of Inherited Wealth: A Social Psychological Perspective," UMI Dissertation Service, Ann Arbor, MI

6   From the unpublished papers of Al Coles and Bill Jahnke, Larkspur, CA

7   "Capital Insight's Bad Bets Caused Losses Of Over $36 Million for Pier 1, Others," *Wall Street Journal*, December 28, 1995, p. A3, and "Goldinger's Bet on Rates Led to Losses Of Up to $100 Million, Associates Say," *Wall Street Journal*, January 2, 1996, p. 2-3

8   Many of the financial coaching procedures described in this chapter are performed by financial experts who are affiliated with The Williams Group

9   From the unpublished papers of Al Coles and Bill Jahnke, Larkspur, CA

12 How You View Your Children

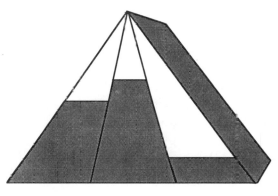

| Preparing
Heirs | Trust and
Communication | Estate/Succession
Planning |

Do you believe that your sons or daughters will have the competence to handle your wealth? If they're like most children, yours have sometimes been irresponsible, and they have made many of the errors that are typical of young people. Has this made you doubt their maturity and judgment? Of course. But, overall, how objective is your opinion of them?

A classic model of the entrepreneurial family unfolds something like this: Dad, who is usually the family entrepreneur, comes home blustering because that is the way he runs his business—giving orders and expecting people to do as he tells them. Dad expects the children to have an adult-level of competence because he is accustomed to that on a daily basis. To a lesser or greater degree, but always to some degree, the children are intimidated by their father even though they love and respect him. They don't undertstand the rules by which he is playing, and how they should react. This is compounded by the fact that they don't get to see too much of him. Feeling intimidated by Dad undermines the children's confidence and lessens their apparent skills in Dad's eyes.

Because she has spent so much time with them, from when they were little, Mom has a sensitive understanding of the children's abilities. She has been a part of the daily trials they have experienced; she's watched how they learned to deal with their peers and how they gradually became more responsible. Mom knows their strengths close-up, and the long, day-by-day struggle it has been for the children to attain them. So, when Mom suggests to Dad that perhaps he is being a bit harsh, that maybe he is expecting too much and is missing some of their good points, Dad would do well to listen. While she may be instinctively downplaying some of the children's faults, she is providing a counter to Dad's critical nature.

The typical entrepreneur, in spite of loving his spouse, tends to view his own evaluation of his children as superior to hers, because she is often inexperienced in business and money matters. Sometimes we'll ask an entrepreneur client, "What do you think of your spouse's ability to manage money and to evaluate your children as custodians of wealth?" The usual response is something like, "Not much." Then we ask, "How much time do you spend each month teaching your spouse how to manage money?" And the reply is "What do you mean, teach money management?" Until we take up the subject, they have never even thought about this.

If Dad keeps his wife uninformed, and he disregards her insights about the children, he is losing a valuable perspective. What we always recommend to Dad is that he begin teaching Mom about money management. The processes I mentioned in the previous chapter, such as family partnerships, are good ways to do this. When Mom has learned some money management skills, her input, together with Dad's, can achieve a proper balance and perspective in evaluating the children. In our experience, this balance works regardless of whether Dad or Mom is the entrepreneur.

When you have acquired a reasonable and balanced view of your grown-up children's strengths and weaknesses, how do you determine whether or not they are capable of handling wealth or of managing a business? One way not to determine this is by allowing your feelings of the moment to be the judge. Not only is that a poor way to decide—it isn't fair to them. An important part of our Integrated Wealth Transfer Process™ is to help families develop measurable and observable standards for their children.

These kinds of standards were lacking in the Tillich family, where Jo Tillich is the CEO of an appliance parts distributorship. Her son, Will, had been managing one of the branch stores and, in a family meeting, Jo blurted out, "Will, I don't think you're performing up to par."

"Hey, mom, wait a minute," he shot back, "as far as I can see I'm doing great. What are you talking about?"

She went on to detail her complaints and then the exchanges between them started to get heated and we intervened.

"Jo, what are your standards for good and bad performance? Are those standards observable and measurable? Are they sound enough that you, yourself, wouldn't mind being measured against them?"

Well, she didn't have objective performance standards—she was annoyed by a longstanding inventory problem that hadn't been adequately dealt with. It turned out that, overall, Will had actually been doing a pretty good job.

But, one result of that family meeting was that Jo and Will, together, did develop observable and measurable standards for his performance, and one year later he received a nice bonus.

What about your own standards for your children? For Example, what formal education requirements, if any, do you want your children to have? What if your daughter has learned to be a competent money manager but doesn't want to go to college? Will you still require her to get a college degree before allowing her a responsible role in managing—and inheriting—family wealth?

Some entrepreneur fathers tend to say, "I built my business without a formal education: my children can probably do the same." Others, who regret their own lack of education (or who feel the lack of the prestige it confers), demand that their grown-up sons and daughters obtain MBA's.

What is more realistic is to look at the actual knowledge requirements for being able to manage family wealth effectively, and to compare these requirements to the personality, aptitudes and desires of each son and daughter.

In setting up standards for their grown-up children, some entrepreneurs require a minimum amount of experience dealing with charities. This led to a conflict between one of our clients, George Seerlock, and his twenty-five year old son, Charles. The conversation went something like this.

At a family meeting, George said to his son, "I would like you to start spending a minimum number of hours each month working with charities."

"Well, Dad, I can't. I'm going twenty-six hours a day as it is. I don't have time for charities now—I'm fighting for survival in my own business."

"I know, Son, but the distribution of large sums in charitable donations each year is a part of what your family responsibilities will eventually be."

"Dad, how much time and energy did you give to charities when you were my age? When did you get active in charities? It was when you got to the point in your life when you had things under control and you had the time to think about it, right?"

"That's true, Charles, but now we're talking about a substantial family inheritance, and you have to understand that charitable activities are a part of the responsibilities of that inheritance. Do you understand what I'm saying?"

We were able to intervene before threats and ultimatums began flying back and forth. We suggested, and helped set up, a reasonable time frame for charitable involvement by George's son. After discussion, the family agreed that Charles would only attend semi-annual family meetings on charitable activities over the next two years, so he would at least have some minimal familiarity with what was happening. After that, his involvement would increase until, after ten years, he would be fully engaged with the family's charitable activities. This elevated the debate from an ego conflict to a practical plan. It set up specific, minimum requirements for George's son to perform in order to begin to share the control of family assets.

In any family, there are bound to be disagreements between parents and their children over what education, life experiences and special skills are required before the young adults are competent to inherit and control wealth. With some families, the parents may insist that a liberal arts education and world travel are necessary before their children have the perspective to use wealth beneficially. In other families, actual job experience with several different companies is the main criterion.

The initial standards that are set up are not the most important thing. After all, standards can be changed if conditions and viewpoints change. But, establishing some standards means that the family has tacitly agreed that there should be some objective way to determine whether or not the grown-up children are competent to receive and use wealth wisely. When standards are in place, conflicts over competence no longer revolve around blame; they force the family to let go of the past and look to future performance.

The importance of observable and measurable standards can hardly be overstated. When standards are in place, it also means that the threat of disinheritance is no longer a weapon that can be arbitrarily wielded in order to assure good behavior and general compliance. Inheritance becomes a guarantee that is tied to specific goals which are reasonable and attainable, and for which sons and daughters can plan and strive.

It's important that standards be realistic. One of our client families had five sons, all of whom were working in various family businesses. During a family meeting, the discussion centered around how successful the sons had been in living up to family expectations. Since zero-error standards had been established, there was no way the sons could succeed. Where the family should have been celebrating their many impressive accomplishments, they were constantly beating themselves and each other with a verbal stick.

Finally, observable and measurable standards become a starting point that stimulates family communication; it's a good opportunity for sons and daughters to express their views.

Some entrepreneurs try to control their children's behavior by use of the entrepreneur's Golden Rule: he who has the gold makes the rules. When the children are small, it usually shows up in control of smaller things, such as, "If you're out past ten o'clock you lose your allowance!" When the children are grown, it may well involve larger issues, such as, "You marry that nincompoop and you lose your inheritance!" In one classic case, a father said to me, "I'm not gonna give my daughter and her husband a penny be-

cause I don't like the - - -! I told her not to marry that guy. He's a -
- - and I don't trust him!"

"How about the grandchildren?" I asked.

"They're the result of that - - - union. To hell with them. I'm
not gonna give them anything either!"

"You mean to tell me that your love is really that conditional?
That you only love your daughter on the condition that she does
what you say? Didn't you raise her to be independent?"

"Well, sure." he said.

"Congratulations," I said, "you succeeded. I can understand
your not wanting to give anything to your son-in-law. Nothing in
the world says you have to like him or give him anything. But do
you mean to tell me you're going to cut your daughter off completely because she married the wrong guy? And look at your
grandchildren. They had no choice in this, did they?"

"Well..." he said. He was softening a bit, and I continued.

"After you're dead, do you honestly think your wife is going
to keep them cut off? If anything, she's going to try to give them
twice as much because she feels so guilty. And who will benefit?
Lawyers and the IRS. And who will be hurt? Your grandchildren,
because there's going to be lawsuits and a lot of bitterness. Now
come on, let's get on with what's real. We can structure things so
that your money follows the line of descendency. Better yet, let's
start educating your daughter and your grandchildren in how to
manage money wisely, so that it will be a blessing and not a curse."

In Chapter 11, I discussed the problem of when to tell the children specific financial information about family wealth. In some
cases a particular son or daughter, even when grown-up, still may
not seem capable of receiving this information. But there is another side to this issue, and it is the deliberate witholding of financial information as a tool to try to control children's behavior.
Like the more blatant form of parental control, where arbitrary
judgments and personal biases are causes for disinheriting children, the deliberate witholding of financial information causes one
of two reactions in the children. Either they grudgingly comply
with their parents' wishes and harbor a strong resentment against
them, or they defy their parents, and both parents and children
are resentful. Here is an example of the comments from one grown-
up child of affluent parents:

"My Father's been telling me if I want to look at the financial stuff any time now it's alright. I think he means it, but when I get there it's so complicated. I never get a direct answer of how much or anything like that. I'm struggling to get the information. I say, 'Tell me how much money I have.' They say, 'It's very hard to compute because so much of it is underground.' I say, 'I bet you compute it when you want a loan at the bank. I bet you can come up with the figures.'"[1]

The subtlest form of controlling children's behavior with money may be partly subconscious. The relationship between Janet Kolski and her grown-up daughter, Carla, illustrates this point.

Carla was starting her own real estate contracting company and she wanted to build a house. She approached her trustee and asked for a $150,000 loan.

The trustee told her,"I already released $100,000 to you last year."

"What are you talking about? I never received anything!"

"$100,000 was released to you. Go check with the accountant."

Carla went to the accountant's office. Sure enough, there was a record of a check written to her in the amount of $100,000. Her mother had neglected to tell her about it and had deposited it into a savings account because she didn't think her daughter needed it and wasn't ready for it. Carla is 38 years old and has four children.

Whose money is it? Another client gave his son $50,000 to keep and to invest as he chose. The money belonged to the son, but his Dad kept close watch over it. "What have you invested in?" "Let me see your portfolio." "Can't you do more than 10 percent?" "Remember, I worked hard for that money." Finally, at a family meeting, his son said, "I don't want this money. It's still Dad's money. If I'm going to get any money, I want it to be my money."

Sometimes, the money remains Dad's money even when that is not his intent. It's not uncommon to hear the wives of entrepreneurs say, "It's my husband's money, it's not my money. He earned it, I didn't." This is after thirty or forty years of marriage and the raising of a family.

Family partnerships and other family financial agreements have to be conditional—that is, the children (and parents) must adhere to the rules. But when parents give money to their children, it is important that there be no strings attached—legal or emotional. Their children have to be free to take risks with it as they see fit. Dad or Mom can advise, when advice is requested, but they have to allow their children freedom to risk, even if there is a possibility that the money will be partially or wholly lost. In practice, the hardest part is not convincing parents of this, but convincing their children that it really is their money, and that there are no emotional liens on it.

Trusts are ironically named. As John Levy puts it, "If I trust my children, why am I putting their money in trust?"₂ Trusts are also subject to misuse, as in the example of the family of Milton Pike. Milton founded and built up a large printing and binding business. He had twin daughters, and he established a trust for the purpose of safeguarding his daughters' inheritance until they reached the age of twenty-one. But when the young women came of age, their father found ways to keep extending the trust. This angered and frustrated them. Finally, when they were both almost thirty years old and had still received nothing, they vented their resentment at their father. They asked, "When will we ever be mature enough, in your eyes, to handle money?" Finally, they hired a lawyer. After several years of litigation, the lawyer managed to break the trust, and the daughters received the money. But it left a legacy of terrible bitterness in the family that continues to this day.

Parents can usually think of several reasons to establish trusts for their children, such as waiting for their maturity, and protecting them from mistakes. Left unsaid is the desire to control their behavior and their lives in general. But, controlling grown-up children and mistrusting their judgment can be a self-fulfilling prophecy—they aren't allowed to take risks, they can't learn from their mistakes and they simply don't mature.

As a parent, it is very important to distinguish between wanting to see certain levels of maturity in your children, on the one hand, and forcing them to do what you think is "right," on the other. One idea we frequently recommend is to create performance-based trusts rather than age-based trusts. For example, instead of having a trust pay out at age twenty one, the first payment can be tied to graduating from college; the second payment might require five years of job experience before payment, and so on.

Family offices often play a large role in trusts, regularly disbursing small amounts to mature adults. But place yourself in this position: how would you like to be fifty years old and still be receiving an "allowance?" More than that, many family offices provide exactly the wrong kind of psychology to the inheritor. It is saying, "We will safeguard your parents' money, and you needn't worry about it or be responsible for it." But what the inheritor really needs is for the family office to be a dynamic and creative partner, and to provide opportunities for growth and increasing competence with money.

The final point of this chapter is the importance of being forthcoming with your children about their inheritance. One client of mine decided to clear the air in this regard and, at a family meeting, he said to his three kids: "I love each of you too much to give you any money." This was a difficult position for him to take. The children reacted strongly to this; they didn't like it. They felt they were being judged unfairly, and that they should have the right to prove themselves competent to receive family wealth. Their Dad's decision may not stand forever, but it did one thing for sure; it made the children sit up and take notice. It was also a catalyst for family communication because there were numerous discussions from that point on.

We don't recommend disinheriting your children. On the contrary, we believe strongly that you should spend the next ten years educating your children to a high level of competence and positive values. If you do this, we guarantee that your children will do a far better job of handling their money than if you leave their education to chance.

Much of this chapter has been about the degree of trust with which parents are able to view their children. Many of the recommendations, such as setting up standards for grown-up children and learning to give without attaching strings, are not easy for the entrepreneurial parent to do. In fact, as much as children have to learn to be trustworthy, Dad and Mom have to learn to give up a measure of control over them. So the question of whether or not your children, when they are grown-up, are really competent and worthy of inheriting family wealth depends not only on what they do, but on what you do, as well.

1   Bronfman, Joanie, Doctoral thesis, "The Experience of Inherited Wealth: A Social-Psychological Perspective", UMI Dissertation Service, Ann Arbor, MI 48106

2   From an unpublished work by John Levy, Mill Valley, CA

Involving Your Family With Your Business

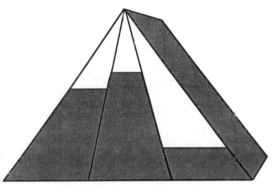

| Preparing Heirs | Trust and Communication | Estate/Succession Planning |

One form of parental control is for parents to make their children's inheritance contingent upon their working for the family business or managing family assets, without considering the children's talents and wishes. As I have said in previous chapters, the true blessing of money is that it provides options. An inheritance should do the same; it should enlarge the inheritors' freedom to pursue what they wish. While a family business and/or family wealth do provide wonderful opportunities for children who are inclined to this kind of life, parental pressure on unwilling children to manage family interests invariably results in unfulfilled lifetimes spent trying to pursue someone else's vision.

On the other hand, a common theme among our clients is where a daughter wants to join the business but is prevented from doing so. This was the case with Leonard Hansen and his two sons and two daughters. The oldest daughter, Holly, was by far the most capable of the Hansen children from a business standpoint, but

Leonard didn't believe that women should run a business. He used every excuse to avoid discussing this issue. When we became involved, neither Holly nor her younger sister were even part of the buy/sell agreement. It took an unbelievable amount of work to get Leonard and his two sons to acknowledge that Holly was a potentially-capable executive; that, at the least, she and her sister should have the option of owning stock in the company. Leonard finally agreed to give his daughters their one-fourth shares in the company upon his death, and that each of them would have a "put" to the company for their shares if they wanted to get out. Leonard still won't acknowledge what a great asset Holly would be to his company, but he's gradually learning to be more open.

What happens when none of the sons or daughters are qualified or motivated to run the business? This is an instance where direct, truthful family communication is vital. When a son, on behalf of himself and his siblings, says to his father: "You know, Dad, none of us are really interested in running the business," that will hurt Dad in the short term. But it lets him know that in the long run he has to find a buyer for the business (or bring in other management with his children on the Board). This makes Dad's life easier because at least the air is cleared and he can plan the direction of the company in preparation for an eventual sale.

The decisions of grown-up children not to participate in the family business aren't cast in stone—they may (and often do) change their minds when they are exposed to the world of business and its challenges and rewards. This is another reason why it is important to follow-up on the methods to promote their involvement which I suggested in Chapter 11, such as teaching your children money management and forming family partnerships. These will make your children well disposed to participating in the family business if they have any aptitude for it at all. In our experience, if you begin this training early—when your children are in their 20's or before—there is a good chance they will want to come on board. If you wait until they are in their late 30's or their 40's, they will probably be past the stage where they are willing to abandon their own careers and learn what is necessary to run the business.

We find it very useful to have the grown-up children of our clients complete questionnaires about themselves and their attitudes toward the family business. We use a separate questionnaire for those sons and daughters who already have expressed a desire to work in the family business and for those who haven't. In the questionnaire for those who want to participate, here are a few samples of the questions asked:

- Do you have a track record of managing other people successfully?

- Do you have a track record of guiding successful projects from conceptualization to completion?

- Are your assumptions and expectations about your role in the family business realistic?

- How would you anticipate providing security for your Mother and Father if and when they give up control?

And here are a few sample questions from the questionnaire for sons and daughters who don't want to participate in the family business:

- Do you know who could run the business if your Father died today (or your Mother, if she runs the business)?

- After your Father is no longer able to run the business, will you be able to monitor the activities of those who manage it?

- What do you think will happen to the company, the family money and other family assets after your Mother and Father die?

The purpose of questions like these is to introduce topics that have typically been neglected or avoided. They encourage both parents and their children to discuss a wide range of issues, from attitudes toward the business to the parents' judgments of their children's abilities.

No matter how perceptive Mom or Dad are, they are so emotionally tied up with their children that it is almost impossible for them to be truly objective about their capabilities without outside help. In fact, the best way to evaluate young adults is to have them work for someone else. This gives the young person a different perspective and it demonstrates how an objective world values his labor. It also insures that he won't receive special treatment or be absolved of responsibilities that other employees have.

After a few years of work experience, several things will have changed for the young adult. He knows that he has to be worth what he gets paid, and if he has only been able to make $15,000 per year, that tells him he has more to learn. But if Dad says "I can only pay you $15,000," and his son has been able to command a salary of $40,000 per year, he can look Dad in the eye and say, "Sorry, I know what I am worth in the world, and if you aren't willing to pay that, I won't come to work for you."

The work experience also allows him to speak with more credibility. If Dad says something that doesn't ring true, he can say with some confidence, "Dad, I've seen a more effective way of doing that." The son is now speaking to his father with credentials given to him by his experience in the business world. This elevates him in Dad's eyes (as well as in the eyes of non-family managers in the business) and it enables him to know that he can make real contributions to the family business. If that son becomes an executive of the family firm, he can compare standards and methods against what he has seen in other companies, and that will make him a better executive.

When, for one reason or another, it isn't feasible for an entrepreneur's son or daughter to find other work, or when Dad sees that some specialized kind of work experience will be an advantage, mutually beneficial arrangements can be made. Several of our clients have asked business friends to hire their son or daughter for a period of time, with two requests: 1) That the Father will pay the salary until the son or daughter actually begins to earn it, and 2) That the child be treated and evaluated exactly as every other employee. This period of testing and tutelage in a friend's company often works so well that, after the training period, the friend is loathe to let the youngster go.

When a son or daughter wants to enter the family business, it is important that observable and measurable standards be established in advance. What are the educational and job experience requirements for the intended position? If it is to be Chief Financial Officer, is a CPA license and/or an MBA in finance required, and must he or she work for the company a certain number of years before receiving the CFO title?

When we work with families, we formalize this procedure of

setting standards by helping family members draw up a "Proposed Policy and Standards for Treatment of Family Members in the Business." This document first defines who are "family members" now and in the future; for example, will step-children and adopted children be given an opportunity to join the business? If so, will they be treated equally with blood-line descendents?

It then outlines a career development plan, with benchmark dates, for each young adult who wants to join the company; it specifies who will be that person's mentor; it determines, beforehand, acceptable performance standards and the rewards and consequences if a young adult does or does not not meet those standards. Further, it establishes "Key Leadership Competency" evaluations in areas such as strategic vision, administrative ability, team building, staff development, productivity, etc.

When the family has completed this proposed standards plan, each young adult (and all other family members) understands what is expected of him or her in terms of apprenticeships, job requirements and job performance. This isolates the young adult's involvement from day-to-day emotional fluctuations and prejudices and provides clear guidance for progress. It also eliminates nepotism.

Nepotism is a common problem with family-owned companies. An example of a classic case is related by Clive Cushman, who manages a large construction company in the Midwest. Clive was hired by the owner to be Division Manager, with authority to make all decisions for that division. But the owner has two sons and he is pushing to get them into the business. He wants his sons to have some supervisory experience and he has asked Clive to let them each be Assistant Managers directly underneath him.

The owner's sons are both capable young men, but they are not as knowledgeable and experienced as other employees in the company. Clive's problem is that if he agrees to let the owner's sons come in at top levels, what kind of a disincentive will that be for the more qualified employees who want those jobs? Also, Clive knows that the owner's sons will only be there a couple of years and then they will move on to start new divisions, leaving him short of trained managers.

If Clive caves in to the owner's demand. he knows that the other employees will resent having the two sons become instant managers, and morale and performance will drop. If Clive resists, he knows he'll be replaced sooner or later. It's a very difficult situation, and it points up the problems that occur when an owner's children are given special treatment.

Jennifer Ames has developed an interesting plan for her son and two daughters. Jennifer owns a large travel agency in Pennsylvania, which she bought several years ago and has built up to thirty-two branch offices. Jennifer began by identifying eight key positions in her company, with definite requirements for each position. Even if all three of her children want to work in the company, there are enough top positions so that there is room for her other employees to advance, as well.

Jennifer wants to retire in a few years. She has enlisted three highly competent businesswomen who own their own businesses to act as mentors to her son and daughters. Each mentor has been guaranteed the opportunity to buy into her company when Jennifer retires. The mentors, in turn, have agreed to teach her son and daughters all aspects of the travel business. Each sibling will work for a year with each mentor. At the end of three years, the mentors will give Jennifer their opinions on the competency of the son and daughters. If at least two of the three opinions on a particular son or daughter are positive, that individual will be given the opportunity of selecting one of the available key positions in the company.

This plan accomplishes several things. It sets standards for Jennifer's children; it gives them broad work experience with three different companies, under expert guidance; it lets them know what they must do in order to get a management position in the family business; and, finally, it provides for an objective judgment of their capabilities.

In training grown-up children to work in the family business, most entrepreneurs forget to impart knowledge that they alone possess. Suppose for a moment that you are one of these typical entrepreneurs. From all of the years you have been in business, you have collected a storehouse of knowledge that is probably not written down anywhere. For example, is it documented anywhere that you have verbally promised the owner of Precision Parts to deliver within 20 days of receipt of their order instead of within the 30 days called for in the contract? Or does anyone on your staff know that Frank Peabody has personally given you a 90-day option to pick up that bargain property across town? This kind of informal knowledge includes all kinds of personal commitments to suppliers agreements with customers; relationships with bankers; and various in-house procedures and operations. You haven't needed these things written down because you know them so well you take them for granted. But if something should happen to you, this knowledge—necessary information that enables the company to thrive—will be lost. Even if you remain active in the business, it will make your children's efforts to learn about the company much harder if they have to extract this information out of you drop by drop.

To help young adults understand how a business really works, and to avoid a possible disaster, we recommend that entrepreneurs begin to keep a log of informal business knowledge. One way the entrepreneur can do this is to keep a reminder on his desk to ask himself, after each telephone call or letter: "Is this something which I have exclusive knowledge about?" If so, he can enter the information into a logbook or into a computer file. This will be of tremendous benefit to his sons or daughters, or to whomever will be running the company in the future.

To briefly summarize the most important points in this chapter

- The more you understand your children's abilities and their own desires, the better you will be able judge what, if any, involvement they should have with the family business.

- The more your children know about your business, the more likely they will be predisposed to becoming involved in it.

- If your grown-up children are interested in working for the family business, encourage them (and assist them if appropriate) to work for someone else for a few years as preparation.

- For those children who are interested in joining the family business, observable and measurable standards for job requirements and job performance, along with a formal career plan, clear the air and avoid most of the problems of conflicts and nepotism.

Your business can provide your sons and daughters with wonderful opportunities that are not available to most youngsters. If you let them see the challenges, the opportunities and the rewards that accompany entrepreneurship, the chances are they will be willing and enthusiastic participants.

14 Estate and Succession Planning

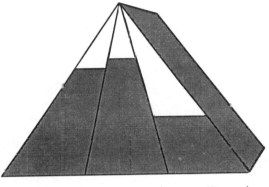

| Preparing Heirs | Trust and Communication | Estate/Succession Planning |

Back in Chapter 1, I stated that traditional estate planning often focuses on Structure—the documents, wills, trusts, buy-sell agreements, family limited partnerships, foundations, etc.—and neglects other important elements of planning. In this chapter I'd like to return to the theme of estate and succession planning.

You'll recall the estate plan determines how family assets will be passed along to heirs and other beneficiaries, and the succession plan determines how the future family business will be controlled and managed. Typically, both are developed concurrently because each affects the other.

Both plans consist of three elements, which are: 1) Mission, 2) Structure and 3) Role.

The Missions define family goals in nonbusiness and business areas; the Structures are the documents that are required to implement the Missions; and the Roles are the parts that each family member will play in implementing the Missions.

Estate and succession planning are incomplete unless they take each of these into acount. For example, here is an aspect of Role that is commonly neglected. If you are the founder of a family business, you are a unique breed of individual. You have demonstrated an abundance of creativity, initiative, determination, boldness, leadership and perseverance—the traits that are necessary to face the challenges of starting a business and building it until it has become a substantial enterprise. But the traits that are required to start and build a business are not necessarily the same as those required to maintain and expand one.

What kind of a business will yours be in the future? When you are no longer active, it is probably reasonable to say that your business will be in an expansion and maintenance phase rather than in a building phase. The history of all the major corporations in the U.S., that have successfully passed from founder to the next generation, shows that the heirs needed skills different from those of the founder. What are the skills that will be needed in your business of the future?

If you are responsible for administering family assets, future skills needed will also change. In addition to working closely with money managers, legal advisers and tax advisers, in the future you will probably have to know more about computers, systems management and international investment requirements, to name a few. So one part of estate and succession planning is looking ahead to try to determine what skills will be needed to manage the family investments and/or business.

In the future, you won't be around to respond to these needs, so your planning must focus on developing the leadership skills of your children and any others who will be responsible for family interests. Developing leadership in others requires a far different skill than displaying leadership yourself. Further, because you won't be around to respond to specific problems, your planning for the future must include developing the kind of structure and tools that will best enable your heirs to respond to problems that arise.

In succession planning, a notorious area of neglect is the founding entrepreneur's reluctance to give up control of the family business. Time after time we have heard clients say that they're waiting for the right time, or that their grown-up children aren't ready yet. This is the case with John Phipps and his two sons. John grudgingly acknowledges that planning for the future is necessary, and he has agreed, in principle, that his two sons will take over his manufacturing business, but he refuses to take any steps to implement it. His two sons, who are now in their late 40's, have been made vice presidents in the company but, in reality, they have no power or authority. When they make decisions, their father sometimes reverses them. The sons are terribly frustrated and are at the point of leaving the company.

John started his company on a shoestring, and one of his most striking attributes has been his dogged independence, which has served him well up to now. Like many another entrepreneur, he feels that he alone has the insight to make things work and that he alone is ultimately responsible for the welfare of the business. John's natural self-confidence deludes him into believing that his past success automatically assures his success in the future.

Also, John is in his 70's and he has lost much of his entrepreneurial energy. At this time in his life, he isn't really interested in developing new products and new markets, while his sons, who are in their prime, want to follow what they perceive as good opportunities. Yet their father never asks for their advice and he doesn't receive it kindly when it is offered. John has already put their love and respect in jeopardy, and he is about to lose his sons' services. The few family meetings that have occurred are confrontational and angry, with Dad in charge of the agenda, and without any prospects for change. The company has consistently been losing market share for the past three years, and sales are down. It is a classic case of the aging and stubborn entrepreneur refusing to face reality, and losing his company and his children as a result.

If John Phipps was able look at his situation objectively, he would see that he badly needs to develop a succession plan. He needs to begin a program of transferring his broad skills and knowledge to his sons while he is still around to do it.

A founder who is easing up on control doesn't need to give up all business activities—there are several important functions he can continue to do for the company as he allows his children more responsibility in running it. But perhaps the hardest lesssons for the mature founder to learn is that his own ideas must now be subject to collaboration instead of simply being implemented. The contribution of skills and knowledge now become a two-way street; the founder's experience and knowledge continue to guide his children, but the newer, up-to-date viewpoints they have acquired are also valuble and need to be acknowledged. The mature founder, who is gradually giving up control of his company, will realize that his strongest contribution is not his continuing day-to-day activity but his role as mentor.

There are many psychological reasons why entrepreneurs and their families resist talking about Dad giving up control of the business. Dad resists because he can't deal with letting go. His whole identity may be based on the business so that he feels lost without it. And the whole subject reminds him of his mortality. Mom and the children don't like to bring up the subject of Dad's easing out because it's uncomfortable for them to speak openly of his eventual retirement and death. It's also awkward for the grown-up children to discuss taking over the business because to talk about it seems callous, and they don't want to hurt Mom and Dad's feelings. Even employees of the company (including those who complain about "management") don't like to think about the owner departing because it means changes and a less certain future with the company.

Here is where the skilled family coach can make a real difference. At a family meeting, the coach may start out by saying, "We haven't covered the issue of what happens when Dad dies; what it will mean to everyone if the business is retained, merged or sold. If Dad dies before Mom (and this is said while Dad is sitting there), is it reasonable that all of the money goes to Mom until her death?"

In the particular family I'm thinking of, the Step-Mom is forty-eight years old, and the two sons, by Dad's former marriage, are forty-three and forty-six. So this question is asking if all the family assets should go to Dad's wife, who is about the same age as Dad's two sons. The discussion continues with the coach's next statement, addressed to the two sons, Peter and Ken.

"Now assume your Dad has left everything to both of you, but with the income going to your Step-Mother. Statistically speaking, your Step-Mom is going to outlive you. Do you know how much of the inheritance you are going to get? Nothing. How do you feel about that?"

"Well," Ken said, "we don't have any choice in the matter.

Whatever they want to do, they'll do."

"That's right," the coach replies, "but let's assume you and your brother do have a choice and you get to have some input into the matter. Should you both have to pay Dad's estate taxes; should we find a way that is less painful; or will you both decide to liquidate the company in order to pay the taxes?"

The coach has introduced several rhetorical questions; no answers are expected at this point—the questions are just for the purpose of getting some of these topics on the table.

The coach continues with, "Peter, let's say that you are going to be running the company and you're going to be earning $200,000 a year. And you, Ken, will only be getting $20,000 a year as a dividend—if Peter pays a dividend, which is unlikely, because of the double taxation. So you're probably not going to get much. What do you think about that? Peter is running the company and earning ten times more than you, even though you both hold equal shares. After your Dad is gone, do you think some resentment might creep in? Would you, at some point, be tempted to say to Peter, 'I want my share. Even if I only put it in the bank, I'd get a five percent return. You're not even paying me that!'"

Meanwhile, during this conversation, Dad is sitting there, enjoying this. The family has never discussed any of this before, and he is very interested in what the boys think. The coach continues: "How can we resolve this? Does it seem right that you, Ken, are locked into company ownership without any income? Or maybe you'd like to work for the company, too. As what? President or Vice-President? If you want to be President, are you qualified? Or put it this way: if you owned the company, would you hire someone with your present qualifications to be President? No, of course not. But who do you think is the best qualified person to run the company? Anyone here? No. So what is going to happen to the company if nobody is qualified to run it? Is it just going to flounder and die?"

Dad is listening, and he would love to hear the answers to all of these questions (which we get to during the course of these meetings). Everyone in the family senses that this is a very important time; that this is something that needs doing. Then the coach continues the discussion on a different tack.

"If Dad dies and you, Peter and Ken, are both running the company, what is your Step-Mother going to live on? Let's assume that the company is generating "X" amount of money and Mom needs more than that. How are you going to pay her? She's not working for the company, is she? Can we put her on the payroll anyway? No, because that's illegal. If you need to pay your Step-Mother a certain amount a year, it's going to cost you an additional amount in taxes. And her income is construed as a dividend, so she will have to pay taxes on the amount she receives. Double taxation. Does that make sense?"

Now the sons are starting to realize how much they don't know. As the discussion goes on in this vein, the coach makes them work at coming to grips with what they think is fair, what they want to do, and how they are going to do it. Then the coach turns to Dad's wife and continues.

"Mom, how secure do you feel about receiving income after Dad is gone? If one or both of the boys are going to run the company, do you feel confident of their abilities to keep it going? Or would you feel safer hiring more experienced persons, not in the family, to run the company? But that shuts out the boys. Is that fair to them? Remember, your future is on the line here. Are you willing to risk your income for the rest of your life on the boys? If not, what would you want to happen before they take over the company? Or would you want to work for the company yourself? If yes, are you, yourself, qualified?"

Hard questions, all of them. And Mom is uncomfortable because she is being placed in an awkward situation. But these are matters that the family must deal with in planning for succession. If these candid give-and-take discussions are avoided, succession can become a crisis, especially when precipitated by the unexpected death of an entrepreneur.

This happened when a friend of mine was tragically killed one night in an auto accident. For all the years he was married, he had never told his wife, Fran, anything about his business—and she never inquired. Fran had been a wonderful wife and mother, but she knew nothing about finances, not even her own checking account.

After her husband's sudden death, Fran sought refuge with friends. They were good people who were looking out for her, but they also knew nothing about business. They told her: "Watch out for your husband's partner. After a partner dies, that's when the other partner takes advantage of the widow." That advice, together with the shock of her husband's death and her anxiety over her financial situation, caused Fran to panic. She began coming to the office each day and questioning the secretaries: "What are you doing? Let me see that," and she would pull the letters out of typewriters and read them. Fran took the company books home for months at a time, even though she couldn't interpret them, in order to give the impression that she couldn't be cheated. Her husbands's partner was very distraught. Finally, he obtained a court order to get the books back, just to keep up the accounts.

Fran continued this kind of behavior, disrupting company board meetings with irrelevent challenges and mistrusting everyone, trying to oversee things she knew little about. One day the remaining partner said to me, "Roy, what am I going to do with her? I'm not cheating her, she's my partner's wife! I'll buy her out and give her all the money I have. I can't stand any more of this." He was right—he couldn't. The strain on him was too much, and he succumbed to a stroke. Without either experienced partner at the helm, the company plummeted and was eventually forced into bankruptcy.

Fran and her husband had a son and two daughters. The effect of all this on them was catastrophic. In addition to dealing with the death of their father, the children have seen the world of business through their mother's eyes, and they are growing up scared and mistrustful of everyone. Fran wasn't unintelligent— her husband could have taught her the basics of business and money management. He could have asked several of his business friends to act as an advisory board to his wife in case something happened to him. Imagine how different Fran's life would have been, after her husband's death, if she had been able to gather together his trusted and knowledgeable friends, and say: "Advisers, help me get through this crisis. Tell me what to do." An advisory team of experienced businessmen or businesswomen to counsel the surviving spouse and children of an entrepreneur is so helpful and effective that we recommend this to all our clients, almost without exception.

The entrepreneur can approach succession as a planned or an unplanned event. The planned event means that he sees himself gradually and voluntarily relinquishing responsibilities for the business, and managing the increasing involvement of his children. Some date in the future has been decided upon for the total transition. The unplanned, or crisis event, means that the entrepreneur intends to work actively in the business and to maintain control until—because of bad health or death—he cannot. At that point, his heirs must be ready to jump in and take command.

The planned succession allows a healthy transition from founder to heirs, and implicit in this transition is a gradual relinquishing of control. The planned succession requires an open, cooperative family environment where all family members are invited to discuss succession issues and to air out their differences.

Planning cannot be done by the founder alone—it must involve family members and outside advisers when needed. The real challenge of effective succession planning is for the whole family to be prepared for whatever events may occur.

The decisions that are arrived at through succession planning are extremely varied. To enable one or more siblings to get out of the family business, a funded, buy-sell agreement may be made, or a second-to-die contract may be created to pay estate taxes. The family may decide to have insurance on Dad, in order to pay the estate tax bill or to buy out other partners if they want to leave the company. Security for the parents is an important part of succession planning.

Brad Burgess, who is a client of ours, and his wife Edna, brought this up in a recent meeting. Brad and Edna are both in their late 50's, and they have two sons who want to take over the family lumber mill. Mike said to me, "Roy, if we turn the company over to the kids, they may take it down the tubes in ten years. In ten years, I'll be sixty-eight and Edna will be sixty-six—we may have another twenty or thirty years to go. What do we do then? It'll be too late to go back into the company."

And Edna said, "We've spent our whole lifetime building up the company. We took lots of risks along the way. Now, I want some security. I want to sell the company."

Sometimes, the best answer is to sell the company. If that is the chosen course, the family should start looking for a buyer now, so it is not a crisis sale after Dad's death. There is absolutely nothing wrong with Dad and Mom deciding to sell the company now for the largest price they can get, and using the proceeds to really enjoy life. Whether the family decides that the business is to be retained, merged or sold, the common theme is still advance planning.

Taxes are very relevant to the issue of planning. The IRS tax code has divided the people who own wealth from the people who will inherit it. Now, Mom and Dad still have the assets—in this case, the business—but the estate has the responsibility for paying taxes on it, and the children, as inheritors, are many times unaware of the extent of this liability. Here's an example, using the case of Hugh and Emy McDowell, and their three children.

The McDowell company is worth about three hundred million dollars. If Dad or Mom dies, all of the estate is passed on to the spouse, tax-free. That's wonderful! "No problems," Hugh tells his children, "There's nothing to worry about. We've got the best law firm and accounting firm. Every document needed has been drawn up. It is all taken care of."

Now if Hugh should die, the scenario will run like this. Emy gets the entire estate. If she receives a modest 5% return after taxes, she has a multi-million dollar annual income. That is more than enough to keep her in the style to which she is accustomed. Time passes, and the grown-up children are now in their late 40's when Mom dies. The business has appreciated; the estate is now worth seven hundred million dollars.

The children seem set for life; they have inherited a seven hundred million dollar business. But now the IRS says: "We want four hundred million in cash for taxes. Oh yes, if you qualify under certain rules for closely-held assets we will allow you to spread the payment over a period of time but you will pay principal plus the prime interest rate. If you are late one day on the payments, it all becomes due and payable that day. The principal payment will be forty million per year, and the interest payment will be another forty million, assuming a 10% interest rate. We want eighty million dollars per year or we want the whole thing now—in cash."

A seven hundred million dollar business is a substantial asset. But have you ever tried to take cash out of a business? It's like squeezing all the juice out of an orange so that the only thing left is the rind and some pulp. How long can a company survive with fifty-five percent debt against assets and all the cash gone?

This is how the tax system works. The lawyers and accountants know it, and Mom and Dad may know it. It's their children who are unaware. One of the questions that this raises is: do parents at least have the obligation to inform their children of the liability of the estate that they will inherit? If they are unprepared, this extraordinary liability will cause profound suffering and bitterness in the lives of their children.

There are other options, and one of the tasks of the coach is to get the whole family together to look at them. One of these options is careful life insurance planning—the lack of it can be devastating, as in the case of Ken Janiewski's family. Ken was a successful entrepreneur—no doubt about it. He had started with nothing and built up a considerable fortune. And while some entrepreneurs are very good at running their business but naive about investments, Ken had this covered as well, and his overall return on investment was enviable. Ironically, it was his successful investing that created the blindspot that was to cause so much pain to his family.

In earlier years Ken had purchased $25,000 worth of life insurance. In hindsight (and ignoring the coverage he had received all through those years) he regreted it. After all, had he invested the same amount in growh vehicles, it would be worth 100 times the original amount.

When an enterprising insurance agent was able to corral him, he'd say, "Go talk to my lawyer or accountant." Then he'd call them first and tell them to get rid of the insurance agent. He didn't want any insurance and he didn't want to be bothered discussing it.

His accountant agreed, saying that if Ken died and the IRS taxed half of his estate, they could use the 15-year payment period allowed by the government to pay off the taxes—no problem.

One of the things Ken loved was flying. He was a licensed pilot and had his own plane. One day, at 15,000 feet, he had a heart attack and lost control of the plane. With him were a key business associate, a customer and Ken's son, none of whom could pilot the aircraft. All four were killed in the crash.

During the investigation into the crash it was discovered that Ken's medical certification had expired—he had been flying illegally, and that created many problems.

Leasing office space had been a significant part of Ken's business. It had been very profitable over the past decade but had experienced some problems due to the recent real estate slump, and the values had dropped by 50% or more. Because Ken had been such a dynamic powerhouse, he had not identified his successor, nor had he completed plans for any family member to learn the business. He was always "going to do it." In fact, he had scheduled it with us several times, but each time he had canceled due to pressing business needs.

His wife of 36 years, Elena, wasn't involved in the business but had co-signed all of the bank's notes. "Don't worry," Ken had repeatedly said, "I have it all taken care of. There's more than enough for you if something should happen."

But after Ken's death, the bank asked for the notes to be paid; there was no one who could fill in for Ken—the one executive who could have done it was killed in the crash—and the bank felt vulnerable with a leaderless business. Then lawsuits were filed for Ken's flying illegally without medical certification. To compound matters, the customer who had been in the plane was the CEO of his own company. That company filed suits for the loss of their key man and the subsequent injury to their business.

Elena was in a bind. She was trying to run the company herself, but she didn't have the needed skills. The atmosphere in the office was that of a sinking ship—aided by rumors of the business's demise, started by competitors. This caused a run of some customers and suppliers. Three of the key executives read the handwriting on the wall and left.

Business properties, although decreased in value, were sold to help pay off the bank loans and other debts. Then the accountants told the widow and the other family members that the IRS wanted ten million for taxes—in installments—but the business could not afford to pay the first year's interest installment of $800,000 and principal payment of $1,000,000.

This whole episode ended in disaster. Ken's lifetime of work building up the business ended with it being liquidated for pennies on the dollar. Elena had enough to live on, but the bulk of the estate was dissipated on lawyers fees, judgments and taxes.

What a different ending this story would have had if Ken had realized the potential consequences of his death and had been willing to use some of his profits to insure his life. Yet for all the logic, getting successful entrepreneurs to do life insurance planning is often a hard sell. One reason for this is because they have seen their parents invest hard-earned money into insurance policies and then "outlive" them. For example, if when dad was young he started paying for a $100,000 life insurance policy, now, at a ripe old age, he sees that he has put in more than face value— maybe $130,000 in payments. He compares these figures—forgetting that he was covered against the risk of his death all of those years—and it looks like a bad investment.

When insurance is viewed solely as an investment it can indeed look like a poor one. Unfortunately, some professional advisers share this attitude, and their short-sighted advice can cause grievous problems.

In fact, careful insurance planning is a highly desirable part of succession planning. An example of this comes to mind in the case of Jordan Neeman. Jordan was 63 at the time and fit as a fiddle. After repeated prodding, he agreed to look at the estate liability figures his CPA prepared and to share them with his family. When they had all viewed the situation objectively, it became apparent that insurance was a necessary part of estate planning, and coverage was purchased and placed into effect.

Five years later, Jordan was on a hunting trip with friends when their jeep rolled over and he was killed. Though it was a terrible tragedy, Jordan's daughters were bought out of the business at the previously-agreed price, his wife had enough income to maintain her lifestyle and those who took over running the business had a cushion to tide them over the period in which they had to pick up the slack. And lastly, there were significant amounts remaining in a last-to-die trust that would pay the taxes after his wife died.

Careful insurance planning had minimized the trauma of this unfortunate accident and averted a disaster for the family.

Another common problem we help solve, with sound estate planning, is how dilution of ownership begets lawsuits. At first, ownership is passed on to a few heirs and further divided when there are many grandchildren, and, eventually, multiple great grandchildren who all own shares. We know one family with 450 shareholders!

When ownership is divided, it is often accompanied by a decrease in interest and knowledge about the business. If, for example, a grandchild owns 1/25 of the family business, but is not actively involved in running it, how much loyalty to the business will he or she have? Will it be enough to allow the business to grow while he or she receives little or no return from that ownership? That is unlikely. More typically, the child or grandchild of the founder says, "I'm not getting anything for my share. I want to see some money."

How knowledgeable about the business will these 1/25 owners be? They are unaware of expansion plans, capitalization needs and possible negative cash flow. Their immediate interests no longer coincide with those of the business. The interests of the founder's grandchildren, who are running the company, are in opposition. They're trying to keep it going and to maintain their livelihoods at the same time. When push comes to shove, the lawsuits begin, and they can be very messy and very expensive.

In one case, a son and daughter and nine cousins were all shareholders in the family business. There was no really important strife between them—just the typical petty conflicts that are common in families. But each shareholder had his own lawyer, his own CPA and his own trust department at the bank. They were trying to run a huge company, but each time a decision had to be made, and one adviser backed it, some of the other advisers had to find some fault with it—they wanted to show they were doing their jobs. The company never expanded because most of its profits were spent on legal fees. Sometimes, this is taken to extreme. In one well-publicized case, the family shareholders were dissatisfied with the company's performance and they fired the grandchild of the founder who was running the company. He filed lawsuits against them, they counter-filed and, to date, both sides have spent twenty-three million dollars in legal fees. The financial costs have been substantial, but the relationship costs have been enormous and will continue for generations.

Pre- and post-nuptual agreements are helpful documents for families, but it is a challenge to create and implement agreements that avoid long-term conflicts. When someone asks their betrothed to sign a document, in case they get divorced in the future, it sends a potentially contentious message—a message that is easily mis-understood. The reaction to it may be: we aren't even married yet and you are planning for our divorce. To help reduce the strong emotions that can accompany nuptual agreements, we recommend several approaches. Here are a few of them:

1) Make it a family policy that everyone signs a nuptual agreement as a tool to protect family partners and family business interests.

2) Reassure spouses-to-be that the family does not think a divorce is going to occur, and explain the reasons for the family nuptual policy.

3) Give spouses-to-be adequate financial information so there are no secrets.

4) If you are going to discuss nuptual agreements at a family meeting, make sure all spouses and spouses-to-be are invited.

5) Inform spouses-to-be of family nuptual policy at an early date, and don't wait until the last minute to ask them to sign.

6) Inform spouses-to-be that their future will be affected by the nuptual agreement, and that they should have their own lawyer to advise them.

Conflict among heirs over ownership or succession is not in-evitable. One of our clients, Jeff Liguori, pursued a reasonable and effective solution to succession in his company. Jeff's business is manufacturing adult games like "Monopoly" and "Scrabble" for the game companies. He owns three printing and manufacturing plants. Some years before Jeff was ready to retire, he began to think about a successor. He had a bright, young son-in-law who was untested; there was the possibility of a nephew and a niece; and there were also two key female executives employed with the firm. They were all good, competent people, but he couldn't make a decision. So Jeff opted for a simple but innovative solution. He gathered all of the candidates together and asked them if they would try, by themselves, to form a succession team.

The mission of the five-member team was not only to choose an eventual CEO, but for each member to gain a familiarity with all aspects of the business so that all of them would be in a position to perform needed supporting roles. It took them two years. Gradually, the team acknowledged that the outstanding leader was the senior female executive. They took another year to confirm their choice by making her acting CEO and monitoring her performance, while Jeff remained in an advisory capacity. It was a terrific win-win solution for all participants. The team worked together so well that they decided to stay intact as a management advisory group, and Jeff was assured of not only a competent successor but an effective support team.

One of the critical times in the transition of control from founder to successor is when the founder disagrees with a major decision of his designated successor. This can be the make-or-break point of the succession. If the founder attempts to rescind his succcessor's decision, he will probably, at the least, lose the support of his successor; at the most, his successor will initiate a battle over control or will walk out.

For an entrepreneur who is planning for succession, it is necessary to put all of the cards on the table. At a family meeting on the topic of succession, we usually ask Dad: "When are you going to retire (we have already asked him in private, weeks prior to the meeting)? Next, we ask: "What will it take for you to feel comfortable that whomever you choose to run the company is competent? Have you developed observable and measurable standards that qualify someone to take over? Is there a family member or company executive you feel has the potential to run the company? If not, how are you going to find someone? If your son or daughter is going to be President of the company, do your employees know this? Have you discussed this decision with all of your key executives and advisers? Will your executives be comfortable with your choice of successor?"

When a succession plan has been developed and everyone has agreed to it, we request a family meeting with all outside advisers present. Then we announce that this is a Succession Fire Drill, and that Dad has just "died" (while he is sitting there, watching).

This is a good way of finding out the flaws in the succession plan, seeing if everyone knows his or her responsibilities, and determining how well the plan is being implemented. It may take some time for this exercise to be completed, or we may run through it several times before everyone has it right. By then, Dad will have gained the confidence that the succession plan will actually work, because he has seen it work.

The Succession Fire Drill is a tremendously powerful tool to anticipate and prevent many succession problems from arising. We recommend it to all our clients and especially to all those persons who believe they do not need to look into these issues.

Effective estate and succession planning take time; they are not an overnight affair. They require the continuing input of all family members, all close advisers and key personnel of the business. They also requires forthright, open communication. Estate and succession planning are ways of anticipating possible future events and predetermining their outcome to the largest possible degree. They are a vital step in the Integrated Wealth Transfer Process™.

Teaching Your Family to Deal With Professionals

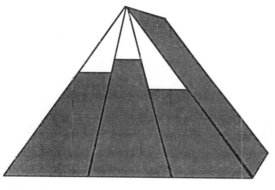

Preparing   Trust and   Estate/Succession
Heirs   Communication   Planning

Hundreds of thousands of pages are added to the Federal Register each year. That's just federal law and doesn't include state, county and municipal legislation and all of the court decisions at every level. This means that there are literally millions of new laws on the books each year. There is no way that you (or I) can keep abreast of how these laws impact your business. We need specialists—those who focus on relatively narrow areas. And so you have a team of specialists on call to assist you. You rely on your attorney for legal matters, on your accountant for tax and audit matters, on your money manager for investments and, if you are running a business, on your executives for business knowledge. If you have a family office, you have advisers who specialize in helping your family manage its assets. But do you blindly accept and implement their advice without thinking it through yourself? No, of course not. You use these advisers as resources to help you make decisions. But what would happen if you weren't around? Would your spouse or your children be able to use this advice as effectively?

Our experience indicates that when the primary decision-maker of the family dies, the family will look for guidance from advisers whom they deem to be either more experienced or smarter. Often, they'll take the will, the buy/sell agreement and other documents to their lawyer and ask, "What do we do now?" The lawyer's first obligation is to look at things from a legal standpoint and provide a legal opinion. Areas outside of the adviser's speciality may not be considered. For example, a sound legal opinion may or may not also be a good business decision. The specialized focus of professionals was clearly spelled out for me when I attended a summer program at the Harvard Law School some years ago. In a class on estate planning, the professor told us that if we had questions, we were to submit them after class and he would address them the following day—he had too much material to teach us to allow interruptions during class time. But by the end of the first week, I had submitted about twenty-five questions and none of them had been addressed. I was exasperated.

When class began in the following week, I stood up and said, "Professor, I submitted twenty-five questions last week but none of them have been answered. Can you tell me when you will be able to address them? They are important to me."

The professor turned to me. "Mr. Williams, I want you to know that your questions have nothing to do with law—they have to do with business matters. They are business questions. If you have business questions, go to the business school. This is a course on law, and that is what we are discussing—not business."

The professor was absolutely, one hundred percent correct. What he was talking about was how to interpret the legal significance of a document. The business impact had nothing to do with it. When a businessman talks to his lawyer about matters related to his business, he usually assumes the lawyer is similarly talking in terms of his business. But the lawyer may not be. While the lawyer may or may not also have business experience, he will be responding in terms of the law. What I really learned from that Harvard law course is that when I talk to a lawyer, I am very much aware that we are discussing law. Since then, when I ask questions of lawyers or accountants, I do not ask them to make decisions about business, family or personal matters.

In estate planning, an often-overlooked distinction is the difference between the plan, itself, and the documents that are meant to implement it. Many lawyers are expert at drafting documents but they may not be able to place family documents in the broader context of the business and personal needs of family members. Someone has to determine the areas in which that expert should operate, and which areas are beyond his specialized focus.

If something should happen to you, the business decision-maker in the family, it's likely that your family members will surrender their authority to a set of credentials—CPA, CFO or VP—and blindly accept an expert's advice. After all, you've probably often said to your family, "I'll talk to my lawyer about that," but you have never revealed to them the fact that you evaluate and sometimes challenge what the lawyer says. You probably haven't said to your spouse and children, "Here is what my advisers told me and, as a consequence, I am going to do this, but I am not going to do that." So your family believes that Dad does whatever his advisers tell him; and they follow suit and literally give up their authority and responsibility for their own future. This is often a dreadful mistake, and the family may pay the price for years to come.

When legal issues are involved, as they almost always are, it is helpful to understand the nature of the adversarial system. The responsibility of your lawyer is to protect your rights, not necessarily to resolve conflicts through nonlegal means. If he or she doesn't protect your legal rights, your lawyer may be liable. This is what our adversarial system demands. The law firm, in order to be certain that your rights are legally protected and that it can't be held liable for mistakes or poor representation, may carry the case to the "nth" degree, with cost as a secondary priority. In the process, important family interests, outside the purview of the law, may be ignored. The most important thing to understand from this is that a lawyer's method of protecting your rights is sometimes not in your best interest.

I recall the case of Winnie Myers and her two sons. Winnie's husband had died two years earlier. For years, he had talked to his advisers alone and had never included other family members in these discussions. After he died, the older son stepped in to try to manage the company. In doing so, he incurred a debt of nine hundred thousand dollars and he was having trouble repaying it. After being served with a notice of default on the loan, Winnie went to her attorney, a very bright, competent man, and asked, "What can we do about the debt?"

"I'm afraid it's going to court," he said. "You signed a continuing guarantee and the bank has filed suit to collect on it. You don't have much choice."

From the legal viewpoint, her lawyer was right. And the suit was justified from the viewpoint of the lawyer representing the bank. But is it in the best interest of the family and the bank to settle the lawsuit in court?

For some lawyers, their sincere perception is that the courtroom is the fairest and easiest way to resolve conflict, and courtrooms are where they can practice their art and earn their livelihood. But our experience tells us that the very last thing you want to do is go to court. Our experience tells us that what is needed is for all the parties to sit down together and negotiate.

When I and another adviser became involved with the Myers family, we were able to get the family and the bank officers to sit down together. When all the facts were on the table, it became apparent that Winnie's company had been a good customer of the bank for a long time and that the company was basically sound. These were factors that hadn't been apparent from the legal documents. In just forty-five minutes, we were able to agree to dismiss the lawsuit and to negotiate payments in such a way that the family business could continue and the bank would feel secure about their loan.

When a family has lost its major businessperson and decision-maker, professional advisers can be very intimidating to the other members of the family. We see this happen time and time again to the families of our clients. The situation is exacerbated when the professionals at a family office tell family members, "You don't have to worry about that—we'll take care of everything." By relieving family members of responsibility, the family office is also keeping them ignorant and powerless. I feel strongly that professional advisers should be helping to educate the grown-up children of entrepreneurs instead of isolating them.

Arthur Britten's family illustrates this point. Arthur owns several carpet mills in Georgia and North Carolina. For years, he has deliberately included his son and his daughter in his sessions with advisers. The son and daughter have watched how Dad deals with them, how he challenges them and how he evaluates their advice. About three years ago, Arthur had a chance to increase the vertical penetration of his market by acquiring a chain of retail carpet stores. It seemed to be a good deal. Arthur's son and daughter were there when Arthur's advisers and the selling parties got together for a presentation. Arthur's MBA business consultant said, "We believe the numbers in this case are right, and the net profit of this venture will be a 20% compound return." Arthur's CFO supported this position.

His adult children, by this time, were experienced in dealing with advisers, and they watched and listened closely. Arthur's children had watched their father deal with advisers for several years. They watched him talk with the banker, the accountant, the lawyer and all the vice presidents, and how he dealt with them all. Over time they developed an intuitive sense of both the skills and the limitations of these advisers. When the presentation for the carpet store acquisition was over, they approached Arthur in private, and his daughter said, "Dad, there is something wrong with these numbers. We don't know what it is, but it's there. They are hiding something." They discussed it further and, although the money was on the table, Arthur decided to back off from the deal. Later, he found out that much of the information presented was fraudulent—even though the accountants had approved it— and the retail chain was in deep trouble.

There is no question that lawyers, accountants, insurance specialists, bankers and other professionals provide a needed resource for the entrepreneur. But too often, the entrepreneur regards these specialists as his personal resource and does not include other family members in his discussions with them. This isolation works not only to the disadvantage of the family but to the disadvantage of the entrepreneur as well. When the entrepreneur meets alone with advisers and they identify a potential problem, it is far easier for him to deny the seriousness of that problem and to avoid corrective action than if other family members are present. We have worked with several clients who have been meeting alone with their advisers for years, and who have yet to come up with succession plans. This neglect would be hard to maintain if all family members were participants.

Advisers are trained to react to your needs in terms of their specialized training, but they are not necessarily trained as business and family decision-makers. From their viewpoint, it may be logical to proceed toward a particular solution, without digging deeply to see if there are optional solutions.

From your own experience as a successful entrepreneur or administrator, you have developed the ability to appreciate and evaluate the advice of specialists, but you have also developed the ability to weigh all options. How will your spouse and children gain your ability to deal with advisers? How will they learn that they don't have to accept advice simply because it comes from a set of professional credentials? By being present when you work with your advisers, they'll learn it gradually, just like you did. And they'll learn it effectively, just like you did.

The team approach multiplies the effectivenes of everyone when all advisers are present at the table. When everyone has the same information, the synergism can be almost magical. The family members learn, the advisers learn and the family ends up stronger.

16 The Results of Estate and Succession Planning

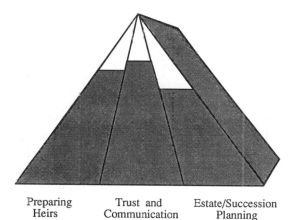

Preparing Heirs   Trust and Communication   Estate/Succession Planning

An important part of estate and succession planning is to look into the future and create the conditions that prevent future conflicts. One aspect of this is trying to assess how control and ownership of your business and assets will affect the lives of your children. In this regard, one of the issues we raise with all of our clients is the difference between treating your sons and daughters fairly and equally. This is a significant point, and I will illustrate it with an anecdote about your two mythical children, Johnny and Janey.

From the time they were very small you, as a loving parent, tried to treat your children fairly. And because they demanded it ("That isn't fair, Dad—Janey got one and I didn't!"), when one child got a new toy the other child had to have one as well. When you found time to play with Janey, you had to make time to play with Johnny. When you went out to the ice cream parlor, they both had to have the same size ice cream cone, even though Johnny was bigger, with a correspondingly larger appetite.

When Janey showed an aptitude for music and started piano lessons, you and your spouse probably felt guilty until Johnny was also receiving some kind of musical lessons, even though he didn't display the same musical talent. In money matters, did you give the children equal allowances (or relatively equal amounts, based on their age) even though Johnny spent his as fast as he got it, while Janey cautiously saved hers? Like most parents, you probably treated your children as equally as possible, not only because the children, themselves, demanded it but because, most of the time, it seemed that equal treatment was fair treatment. Sometimes there were exceptions. For example, when Johnny made the football team and needed a uniform, cleated shoes, and pads, you didn't run out and get the same things for Janey.

Most of the time these decisions were fairly easy to make, based on common sense and the needs of the moment. But sometimes these kinds of decisions can be more complicated. For example, if Johnny was involved in an auto accident and incurred $100,000 in medical bills that weren't covered and for which you ended up having to pay—would you feel obligated to give Janey $100,000? No, of course not. Or would you consider reducing Johnny's inheritance by $100,000? Probably not, you say, because it was an act of fate and not Johhny's fault. But what if it was proved that the accident was caused by Johnny's reckless driving? Would that affect your decision? In terms of their respective inheritances, what is fair?

Let's advance the time frame a few years. Johnny and Janey have grown up. John has been running your company for about ten years and has done a good job—he deserves to be President. Jane is not active in the business but she is a wonderful daughter. On several occasions, when your wife was ill, Jane left her own family to come and care for her selflessly. You love both of your children very much, and you set up their inheritance so each will receive half of all assets. More time passes and your adult children now own the company. John still runs it. He has a satisfying career and a substantial salary. The company is growing, profits are being reinvested and, because of this, no dividend is being paid. Jane has no quarrel with her brother running the company and getting adequate compensation for doing it, but she and her husband are having money problems. Jane knows that the company is now worth millions of dollars and, although she owns half of it, she is not receiving anything. She wants her share or, at least, she wants the income she could get from her half. She perceives that the present arrangement is not fair.

But the company can't generate that kind of cash and John and Jane can't agree on what to do, so lawsuits are filed. The courts finally force liquidation of the company, and both childrens' families part with bitterness. All your years of effort and your hope that the company will continue to flourish—all disappear in a cloud of rancor and a family divided.

This is not a fanciful projection—we've seen it happen time after time. But it doesn't have to be this way. The solution is available; it is to create a far-sighted succession plan that treats each sibling fairly, anticipating their future needs and desires. There are many different ways to rationalize the distribution of responsibilities and perks, but if you ask the question, "Is this fair?" it cuts to the quick of the situation. It also means explaining the plan openly to all of the children and, if they are married, to their spouses.

Let's return to John and Jane, now having grown up and inherited your business. This time, your far-sighted succession plan included sufficient liquidity to fund a binding buy/sell agreement (which we can call a "put"). This "put" now enables Jane, should she choose, to sell all or part of her share with a predetermined payment schedule which will not threaten the company. In this way, both John and Jane win, and the company continues to prosper. Your succession plan has also considered John's and Jane's children, and has established observable and measurable standards for any of them who want to enter the business. It includes job descriptions, educational requirements and compensation levels (subject to future conditions). Because of this, your grandchildren all know where they stand and can consider their opportunities without envy of each other.

One of our tasks as family coaches is to look into the future and point out aspects of succession that result in fair or unfair treatment. These considerations then need to be addressed in open communication during family meetings, until there is a consensus on what constitutes fairness. The final result is a succession plan that goes beyond the concept of equality and which is perceived by all as fair.

Another necessary element in an effective succession is for all members of the family to understand and respect the distinction between ownership, control and benefits. When understanding and respect for these are absent, trouble isn't far away. For a founding entrepreneur there is little need to acknowledge these distinctions—you manage your business, you own it and you gain the rewards from it. But for the spouse or children, the distinctions are important, as in the case of Jack Lamb. Jack had created a succession plan that gave 50% of his company to his wife, Jeanne, in the event of his death. It was hard enough to get Jack to do that because he didn't like thinking about his own mortality. Although he was urged to explain to his wife the responsibilities and limits of company ownership, he never did.

It was left like that for many years. When Jack died, Jeanne had no idea what her role as a company owner should be. She had dearly loved her husband and she wanted to do her best to maintain the company he had built up over the years. But since she knew almost nothing about running a company, Jeanne overcompensated for her naivete by trying to exert control over company operations. For example, when an employee was fired he went to Jeanne and had her intervene with management to get his job back. As a member of the Board of Directors she can't legally control day-to-day company operations, but her constant interference in them is making life miserable for management.

Jeanne has no idea of what is required to sustain the profitability of a large company. Two of her key managers have become fed up and have quit and, as a consequence, market share and profits are declining. She has been repeatedly told by her managers that ownership of a company doesn't necessarily mean control, but she has never been told that by anyone whom she completely trusts. If Jack, while he was alive, had included his wife in planning sessions about the future of the business, and if he had taken the time to explain to her what he wished her role to be, she would have known what was expected of her and what to leave alone. This could have been done very easily, even without business experience on her part. But because it was not done, a fine company is being ruined.

Succession planning has to include a thorough airing of the responsibilities of ownership and control. When the spouse and the children are involved and informed, and there is family agreement over their individual roles, each one knows what to expect as a result of succession.

The benefits of ownership, such as dividends and the value of shares, are relatively easy to spell out in a succession agreement; the benefits of control are more varied and widespread, and their psychological impact is less easy to predict. Benefits that derive from control of a business include more than salaries, bonuses and fringe benefit packages—they include all of the perks that accompany top management. In Rayna Stilson's family, the perks caused problems even though the succession plan had been agreed to by all of the family members.

Rayna had three sons, each of whom shared ownership after her retirement. Her middle son, Howie, was the ablest and most interested in running the company, and he was made President. The other two sons had good jobs with other companies, and they agreed that Howie should run the company. He ran the company for about seven years, during which time the value of the company approximately doubled. By the end of that time, Howie was earning a substantial salary and drove a luxury company car. Twice each year, he took all of the salesmen on company-paid trips to Hawaii. He had a company-funded country club membership as well as a liberal expense account. Whenever all three sons and their families went out together, Howie picked up the company-paid tab.

The other two sons saw that Howie was able to live in a lavish life style and they were not, even though they were all equal owners. They protested and asked for similar perks, which were not granted because they were unearned. Finally, in spite of their mother's strong protests, lawsuits were filed. They have dragged on and there has been no conclusion except that a lot of money has been wasted and the brothers have become perpetual adversaries.

My point here is that, in succession planning, there needs to be a good understanding of what it means to control a company—not only in terms of responsibilities and performance, but in terms of all income and other benefits. Otherwise, envy and its resulting quarrels are frequent.

Deciding who will own and control the business in the future is often difficult for its founder. If the succession plan calls for the company to go to Mom in trust, in order to avoid estate taxes, then Mom controls it and votes the stock. But if the sons and/or daughters are actually running the company, all kinds of personal issues can become enmeshed in company operations. In one extreme instance we heard of, where a widow owned the company, she shouted at her son, "You didn't come over to see me this weekend—I'm going to fire you as President!"

When a spouse has all the voting power and the persons managing the company have no authority to make changes, it is an almost certain recipe for problems.

Often, Dad, in choosing a successor, either doesn't want to hurt his children's feelings or he is caught in a web of perceived family expectations. In the case of Hugh McDowell, it was assumed that Hugh would retire and his eldest son would become President. The younger son would become COO. But Hugh kept putting the date off; he wouldn't sign the wills and other documents the lawyer and the CPA had prepared, and no one could get him to act.

When I met alone with Hugh, he finally opened up and said he felt the younger son would make a better President and run the inside, and the elder would do better handling the outside sales, marketing, etc. He also did not want to implement the plan because if he retired and the boys didn't do well, his own financial future would be at risk and he would be too old to come back in and save the company.

When we met with the two sons, they had no difficulty with the management issues. The younger son said, "I don't need to be President. I already run the company from a practical standpoint, and my brother and his wife need him to be President. He does what he does in marketing and sales, and we both agree to let each other do what we do best.

The two sons later confirmed this at a family meeting. So the problem of who to choose as successor was no problem at all—except in their father's mind. In addition, to alleviating their father's anxiety about becoming impoverished, the sons agreed to borrow a sum against company assets and give it to their parents as a retirement fund.

Although the problem is oversimplified in this telling, the main elements of a solution for the McDowell family were resolved in a single evening. It resulted from creating an atmosphere where each persons's interests and needs could be clearly communicated.

It is important for you, the entrepreneur, to share your thoughts and feelings about succession with all other family members (and with others outside the family, if they are candidates for successor). You may temporarily disappoint and discourage those who aren't included in the list of potential successors, but, in fact, by communicating your thoughts, you will be doing each person a service. Moreover, you may be surprised by their reactions and by alternate ideas that they can contribute. As in the example of Rod and Phillip Mcdowell, siblings, and even cousins, often prefer to share responsibilities and control of the business. The top job is not the only job in the business. Other positions can be made very attractive with the inclusion of benefits and incentives. Also, because entrepreneurial families tend to have investment portfolios outside of the business, management of these nonbusiness assets can be a challenging and rewarding alternative to running the business.

Sometimes, when there is more than one competent successor, the best solution may be to split the business into separate divisions, or to buy another business in order to provide more leadership opportunities, or to simply follow the wishes of the children. This kind of openness brought about a good result in the family of Elmo Budd. Elmo owned a large brewery, and his son and daughter were both competent but couldn't work together. Elmo was at a loss about what to do, so I suggested he ask his son and daughter to work out a possible solution by themselves. His son, Allen, wanted to take over the brewery; his daughter, Nattie, really wanted to start her own temporary help agency, specializing in computer services. At a family meeting, Nattie said, "My brother gets to run a company of his own—why shouldn't I be able to have my own company, too?" As a result of that meeting, Nattie, with some help, developed a sound business plan for her agency. Elmo and his children got together with their lawyers and accountants and figured out the best way to borrow enough to fund Nattie's business start-up. Today, both the brewery, run by the son, and the computer service agency, run by the daughter, are doing well.

With clear communication and a measure of flexibility, it usually becomes evident that there are opportunities for everyone. The strongest reason for early communication about succession is that it will clear the air and prevent the backbiting and negative intrigue that flourish in a climate of secrecy. The strongest antidote to succession rivalry, among siblings or between family and nonfamily aspirants, is to let everyone who is involved know your intentions.

Sometimes, when an heir is not competent but is chosen to be successor in spite of his limitations, an existing business employee may take on the actual responsibility of running the company and the heir will be a figurehead successor. This is workable if the actual nature of the arrangement is made absolutely clear to the heir and he agrees to it; if the actual nature of control is left vague so that the heir believes he is really in charge, it is a recipe for disaster. Also, the compensation level should reflect the real situation. If, for example, a Vice President is actually running the company, he should receive a salary and benefits that are commensurate with his actual responsibilities.

It is important to test potential successors until you are quite confident of their ability to do the job effectively, before formally naming them. Once one or more successors have been named, and those persons begin to take on appropriate responsibilities and gain a measure of control, it is very difficult to revoke your decision.

When choosing a successor, take a look at your own entrepreneurial skills. How long has it taken you to acquire all of them? Twenty years? Thirty years? How many years are you allowing your successor—your son or daughter or whoever it is going to be—to gain all of these skills? If you wait until you're seventy or more, your sharp, talented son or daughter isn't going to remain available that long. And if you're seventy, will you have the energy, the determination and the patience to train him or her? It takes time to train someone properly, especially to acquire all of the varied skills needed by an entrepreneur; it may require ten to twenty years. Furthermore, your decision on one or more successors is going to have an impact on which way you take the company; how it will be structured and whether it will be retained or sold. Too many times, the family entrepreneur waits until he is seventy or more years old to make a decision on succession—a decision that should have been made when he was between forty and fifty.

Now is the time to ask yourself:

- Have your children demonstrated the required competence to manage your company and your wealth?

- What observable and measurable standards are you using to evaluate this? (Standards were discussed in Chapters 8 and 12)

- If your children are not presently competent, has everyone agreed to a procedure for them to become competent?

- If you died today, will your heirs benefit from your estate or will it become a burden and a source of conflict?

Where large family assets have remained intact through succeeding generations, it can usually be traced to heirs who retained stock while giving up incremental control. Sometimes, this happened by the eventual dilution of the stock over time through public offerings. Or the family chose to use professional managers while maintaining seats on the board to make sure that family interests were not ignored.

A succession decision obviously affects the company employees. If you decide to turn your company over to one or more of your grown-up children, or if your succession decision hasn't been made yet, how committed will your key executives be? If I am one of your executives, I know that if the company goes public or is sold, a new management team will probably be coming in. Why should I commit myself to staying with the company? The only way I will commit myself is if I know the company is going to remain intact and I have some promises—from you.

Retaining key executives; avoiding fights between heirs; naming your successor; allowing your successor an adequate number of years to learn all the necessary skills; treating your grown-up children fairly as opposed to equally. These are just a few of the many compelling reasons for squarely facing all of the succession issues now, while there is time and energy to do it right.

The Right Kind of Assistance

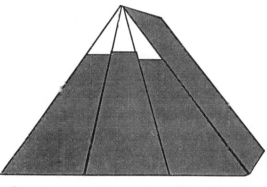

| Preparing Heirs | Trust and Communication | Estate/Succession Planning |

What is a family coach? In previous chapters I've given several examples of some of the things a coach does. There are many others. The job is something like being a movie producer. A movie producer wears several hats, including that of planner, comptroller, logistics coordinator, mediator, etc. The producer is the one who has expertise in a number of areas and who brings the whole package together and makes it work. Similarly, a family coach wears several hats: estate planner, succession adviser, communications specialist, family counselor, etc. Like the producer, his task is to help make the whole thing—the family—work together.

The movie producer must be careful not to allow his personal vision of the completed work to impede the talent and creativity of the director, the scriptwriter, the cinematographer and the actors. Similarly, the family coach must be careful not to sway family values and goals, and to never usurp the authority of family members. He is there to help articulate the family's vision as they define it.

In estate planning, the common vision is to prepare assets for inheritance. But the family coach helps broaden that definition. The estate plan should insure that the children of clients are prepared to inherit wealth and use it wisely. In fact, across the whole spectrum of estate and succession planning, an effective coach introduces new ideas and ways of looking at problems so that entirely new options can be considered by the family.

The coach addresses the personal, as well as helping to coordinate the business and legal aspects of the family. In the process, he will help the family to create an atmosphere of trust that enables sensitive topics to be approached safely. With this kind of mutual trust, questions such as, "Can you objectively evaluate the competence of each of your children to manage family assets?" Or, "Since you love your family, why does the business so often receive priority over spending time with them?" Or, "If you are avoiding preparing for succession, what do you think are the real reasons for this?" Or, "Would your spouse know what to do in the event of your sudden death?"

The coach must raise and bring to the table gut-level issues because they have a powerful impact on any plan that is going to be prepared. These are all sensitive issues and, frequently, family members are so wrapped up in their patterns of relating that an objective outsider is needed to resolve underlying conflicts. As that objective participant, the coach must be able to span all of the relevant issues and bring his experience to bear on everything from sibling rivalry to tax law.

In addition, the family coach helps clarify family goals, makes financial data easily understandable and helps the family to develop a series of observable and measurable standards for heirs.

It's important to understand the difference between a coach and a teacher. A teacher conveys knowledge so that you can understand that knowledge and speak it. A coach goes a step further—not only are you able to understand and speak the knowledge, you are able to act on it, to use it effectively. A competent coach should be able to demonstrate a step-by-step plan of how your family is going to reach its goals. In addition, the coach's plan should provide for periodic evaluation of progress in your family—progress acknowledged by you and other family members—not by himself.

The family coach does not replace traditional advisers; he helps integrate their advice into a comprehensive plan that is designed to implement the goals of individual family members, as well as the collective goals of the family.

Nevertheless, for all the leadership that the coach provides, it is worth repeating that he is not there to determine family values and goals—he is there to empower the family to do these things themselves.

How do you find a competent and effective coach that is right for your family? As of this writing, there are not many individuals who possess the cross-training and experience required. But among those who are effective coaches, basically the same rules apply as for finding competent and effective lawyers, accountants, money managers and other advisers. So let me suggest a few steps for hiring advisers in general. First, I suggest that you and each of your advisers jointly develop a job description of what you want accomplished and in what time frame. If you don't provide your advisers with clear guidelines and priorities, you will probably be wasting a lot of time and money as your advisers attempt to guess what you really want from them.

Selecting the proper advisers is very important. To give you an idea of what is involved with the selection of advisers, I'll use insurance advisers as an example. In one instance our client's best friend was an insurance agent with thirty years' experience—a CLU (Chartered Life Underwriter), a ChFC (Chartered Financial Consultant) and, in general, a fine person. In other words, all the credentials that you'd think were necessary. The problem was lack of the right kind of experience. That agent had serviced his clients well but the bulk of them were in the $100,000 to $1,000,000 net worth category. Our client had a substantially higher net worth. When we looked at our client's insurance coverage, we saw that his coverage was sound but it was costing him far more than necessary. We introduced our client and his tax and legal advisers to an appropriate insurance specialist. In a short time he was able to show the client how he could save most of the $100,000 per year in income taxes to pay for the life insurance, and how he could also save most of the $100,000 in gift taxes!

Many of our clients initially think of insurance as a simple commodity—you find the highest degree of coverage at the lowest cost. But life insurance policies are very complex and are by no means uniform from company to company. At The Williams Group we work in close partnership with the largest buying syndicate for life insurance in the world. To illustrate how this relationship can be of benefit, another client of ours, Janet Caine, had purchased life insurance from a local agency. On its face the policy required payment for ten years. But, during the ninth year, the insurance carrier informed her that because of a drastic downturn in interest rates she would have to continue paying for fourteen more years! When we became involved, our insurance associates were able to include our client in a negotiation with the carrier on behalf of a large number of policyholders. The clout they were able to apply reduced the extra payment period from fourteen to three years—a very significant saving.

What I want to get across here is that the selection of the right advisers is itself a sophisticated process that requires considerable experience in working with these specialists. It's also worth repeating that it is important you choose people with some experience at your level of net worth. For example, a lawyer or accountant who is only experienced with estates of several hundred thousand dollars will generally not have competence dealing with five million dollar estates; and the adviser who is experienced with fifty million dollar estates may not have the expertise to work with estates of several hundred million dollars or more. Each level of assets presents a different ball game that requires experience at that level.

No matter what expert you hire, you have to make sure that their experience matches the nature of the work to be accomplished. For example, a client who was involved in a lawsuit hired a lawyer who was the most notable and recognized expert in his field. His knowledge was exemplary. However, he had never won a case—as a trial attorney, he was a disaster. The client should have hired a competent trial attorney and used his "expert" as a resouce or expert witness. By not determining the trial competency of the expert beforehand, several million dollars was lost.

Another thing to look for in advisers is their ability to be team players. This is essential because much of their responsibility will be to work with other advisers. We have seen too many occasions when an individual has exhibited initiative, creativity, independence and follow-through but has simply not had the ability to coordinate his efforts with others.

At The Williams Group we counsel all of our clients to check out and personally talk to all listed references. It is amazing how often references are not checked, with the result of incompetent or innappropriate advisers being hired. We ask our clients to interview all adviser-candidates personally, and to get to know their personal values.

In addition to requirements for professional advisers, there is another special requirement for a family coach, and that is your feeling about working with him. No matter how impressive his credentials, if you don't like dealing with him, pass him up and find someone you do like.

One of the roles of the coach may be to help find other advisers with whom all members of your family are comfortable. In the final analysis, mutual trust is the absolutely essential ingredient between you and your advisers, and your own intuitive sense will be your guide.

At the beginning of this chapter I said that a coach brings to your family a broad expertise which covers estate planning, tax analysis, management, succession planning, family counseling and a host of related areas. With this expertise, the coach will be able to translate the personal values of your family members into an effective, far-sighted, wealth transfer plan. As your family implements this plan, a wonderful side-effect will be occurring: the level of trust and cooperation within your family will be rising dramatically, and you will acknowledge that your family has become a team.

The Challenge of Relinquishing

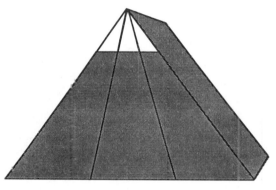

| Preparing Heirs | Trust and Communication | Estate/Succession Planning |

Sometimes, it's very hard to give up control of a business or other asset, even when you know you should and you've given your word that you will. Arthur Britten recently went through this. Art has several broadloom mills near Atlanta. He has two very capable children—his son, Macon, and his daughter, Deirdre—who were in their mid 30's when this lesson began playing itself out. Both of his children were anxious to take over more business responsibilities and when we met with the family, Art said he thought that they would be ready to take over one of his companies in about five years. I asked Art, "Why the five years?" and he cited several skills that they needed to acquire, and some specific experience he felt they needed.

"So," I continued, "it's not really the time element that's important, it's the skills and experience level of your children, right?" I encouraged Art to draw up a list of requirements—observable and measurable standards—for specific objectives they would have to meet before he would consider them ready. No time limits were placed on his children meeting these requirements. Art made up the list, and he gave his word that he would turn one of his companies over to his son and daughter once his conditions had been met.

With this agreement in hand, Macon and Deirdre worked very hard at learning what was necessary. To Art's surprise, instead of taking five years to meet his conditions, they did it in two years. Faced with the reality of letting go one of the four companies he had built single-handedly, Art started waffling and it wasn't clear that he was going to live up to his word.

Art went through some powerful emotions over this, and he realized how hard it was for him to let go of something he really valued. At one point I advised him, "Art, you've got to follow through on your commitment, or you'll lose your credibility with your children, and your relationship with them will really suffer. Is the business worth that?"

Finally, he came through and he made Macon President and Deirdre CFO of his Dalton, Georgia mill. To his credit, Art left them alone to run it their way, giving advice only when it was requested. The first year of his children's management was unprofitable, but by the last quarter of the second year, they had turned it around and produced a break-even business. The third year they hit a home run.

Actually, Art had a relatively easy time of it; he was still actively managing three carpet mills. When an entrepreneur tries to let go of a single business, much more is at stake, including a loss of identity. Often this letting go happens abruptly, because of illness or some other unplanned-for event. In these cases, there has been no preparation, and the entrepreneur doesn't have time to build a new self-image. Feeling lost and empty, he may (often subconsciously) sabotage his successor.

Witholding required knowledge or authority from a successor is a common and well-known phenomenon among retiring entrepreneurs. It can occur regardless of whether the successor is brought in from the outside, is an employee of the company or even is a son or daughter of the owner. It's just hard to let go.

Another client, Bob Oliver, seemed more enlightened. He decided to retire at age fifty-eight from his foundry that produced precision turbine blades for rocket motors. Bob promoted his Vice

President for Marketing to the role of CEO. Then Bob and his wife spent the next six months traveling—something he'd never had time to do before.

When Bob walked into his old office, after being gone for six months, he was shocked to see that his pictures weren't on the wall behind his desk. His several plaques had been taken down. The whole office had been rearranged. Bob was outraged. He bellowed at his old friend, "How dare you take down my pictures! Who do you think you are? Because I named you President doesn't give you the right to re-do my office!"

The man who was the recipient of all this anger was so taken aback he couldn't speak. As far as he knew, Bob was retired and gone. He couldn't figure out why all the hostility was coming at him.

Later, Bob apologized to his President and confided to me that when he saw that his things had been removed, he was just devastated. He said it was one of the most painful times he could remember—the feeling of not being needed anymore. It wasn't true, of course, but what he was feeling was real.

There are many reasons why entrepreneurs hesitate, prolong, and even come back out of retirement. The reasons include loss of identity, lack of contact with close business acquaintances, sheer boredom and lack of confidence in successors ("What if my kids fail? What do my wife and I do for income?"). When a retirement date gets close, what I hear often is, "Roy, I've been reconsidering," "Roy, I've just got a few things I want to tidy up," "Roy, I just need to get through this quarter." Underneath these casual rationalizations, the entrepreneur is frequently terrified.

There are several things we recommend our clients do to smooth the transition to retirement. For example, when Mary Petreska retired as CEO of a large construction subcontracting firm, she retained a small office and a modest, symbolic salary from the company. Mary shows up once or twice a month to help the company make use of her many personal contacts. She has her desk to go to, an active file of contacts, and old friends to see at the office. This arrangement is a win-win situation; Mary doesn't interfere with day-to-day operations, the company makes use of Mary's knowledge and she still feels needed.

What we emphasize most to each of our clients is the importance of preparing ahead of time for retirement. Here are some of our suggestions.

- Plan a specific future date for retirement, announce it publicly and stick to it as if it was inviolable.

- Maintain some minimal form of involvement with the business. In many cases, becoming a member of the Board, or Chairman of the Board, is an excellent way to broaden your perspective without having to be involved in day-to-day activities.

- If possible, arrange for necessary retirement income to come from outside the business, so your life style doesn't depend on your successor(s).

- Retain a physical office and a secretary to keep up your files and handle correspondence, etc.

- Plan ahead of retirement with several non-business interests to keep you occupied. Consider involvement with philanthropy or make use of the prodigious knowledge you have acquired over the years by teaching (formally, at a college, or informally, through community groups).

- Be prepared for the possibility of a certain amount of temporary depression. This is a major change in your life, and it isn't always easy, in spite of preparation. Be aware that this may be a difficult re-orientation period, and seek professional help if it becomes overwhelming. Consider contacting SCORE (Service Corps of Retired Executives) which is a group of retired CEO's who provide support.

In Chapter 7, I presented a system—called the Five Equities—which enables you to clarify personal values, and short- and long-term goals of each family member, plus those for the family as a whole. Approaching retirement is the time to reevaluate these values and goals; to see how far along you are to reaching your own goals, and what are the next steps to bring them to fruition.

A lack of retirement planning usually creates problems with the entrepreneur's family, with employees and with the entrepreneur, himself. Lack of planning can also shorten the retiree's life. Actuarial studies by insurance companies typically show a brief life span for a retiree who does not remain physically or mentally involved.

Retirement can be a time of wonderful opportunities. For many entrepreneurs, who have spent much of their lives tending the business almost exclusively, retirement is a time to begin tending their total lives—something they have never before had the time, the energy or the money to do.

And lastly, timely retirement is an integral part of the process of preparing your grown-up children and grandchildren for inheritance; it gives them the opportunity and incentive to build on your efforts while they are at their peak of performance and interest. Personally, I can think of nothing more pleasurable than to spend time with my grandchildren. I hope you feel the same. Your values and actions will be a beacon to guide them in many ways—some of which you can see and some you cannot.

19 Choosing the High Road

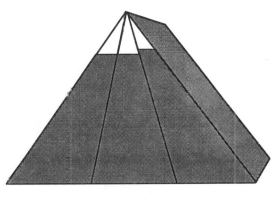

| Preparing Heirs | Trust and Communication | Estate/Succession Planning |

In the classic play, All My Sons, by Arthur Miller, a manufacturer is caught up in an ethical dilemma. The time is World War II, and he has a contract to make precision parts for U.S. warplanes. He is behind schedule and is facing strong pressure to meet his quota, but the latest batch of parts have come through with defects. This entrepreneur is generally honest and patriotic but the pressure on him is intense.

The parts are urgently needed. If he rejects the parts, delivery of the planes will be held up, he will lose the contract and he will sustain a huge loss. If he ok's the parts, there is a chance that they will fail, leading to the possible loss of pilots and planes. The play is made more dramatic by the fact that the boss's own son is an Air Force pilot.

He decides to approve the defective parts and ship them. As the play leads to its conclusion, the man learns that his own son has been killed when his plane crashed, due to his own defective parts. The man's role in shipping the defective parts is exposed, and his life collapses around him in ruin.

While the high drama of this play is a relatively rare occurrence, over the years I have noticed a creeping tendency in our society to overlook the ethics of a situation in order to reap a short-term gain. This tendency is noticeable in some prominent business schools, where the prevailing ethos seems to be to maximize profit, regardless of the consequences. It's as though making money has become an end in itself.

There are many occasions when a short-term gain can be made by ignoring the ethics of the deal; and sometimes lean times make these gains very compelling. But as anyone who has been in business for a length of time knows, the "high road"—that is, the road of ethics, integrity and generosity—is the only way that will insure long-term success.

My own personal opinion is that the world of commerce is not exempt from the spiritual laws that govern our lives. From my own experience, I am convinced that there are basic principles that impact upon the businessman or the manager of wealth. I have found, for example, that whatever your actions, they will often attract like actions back to you; if you are committed to taking advantage of people, the world will respond by providing you with ample opportunities to hurt yourself. If you go out of your way to help others, you, too, will receive help—often from unexpected sources.

There seems to be an organized system of energies in the world that respond not only to what we do but to what we think, as well. I believe the best way to harmonize with and make use of these energies is to follow your heart—follow your own sense of what is right, and make sure you are not hurting anyone else in the process.

I know that I am not saying anything new here. If you are an experienced entrepreneur, you have, no doubt, been through many, many ethical tests in your own life. This kind of experience is not something you learn in school—it comes from years of making tough choices and living with them. I call this kind of accumulated knowledge, "wisdom." My main purpose here is to encourage you to share your wisdom with your children.

In my own life, I know that my children are my greatest asset. Were they also my greatest headache? Yes, that too. Would I do it all over again if I had the chance? Yes, and I'd have more children, because they are the greatest achievement of my life. But, most importantly, I would again make sure that I encourage my children to choose the High Road. If this single task is done well, most other things will fall into place. What more profound legacy could we possibly leave our children and grandchildren?

20 Completing the Process

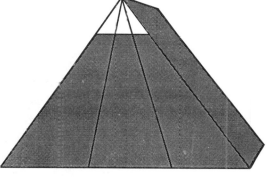

| Preparing Heirs | Trust and Communication | Estate/Succession Planning |

Throughout this book I've emphasized that our Integrated Wealth Transfer Process™ is not a quick fix. It isn't something you can start tomorrow and finish next week. It requires a strong and continuing commitment from you and from your family.

In describing this process, some of the questions I've raised are: What is your relationship with your children? Are family members able to communicate openly and candidly about their concerns? How prepared are your children to manage the business and other family assets? Have you established observable and measurable standards that will enable you to evaluate their competence? Will their inheritance provide them with opportunities to enhance their own lives and the lives of those around them, or will it be a destructive burden to them? Are you doing everything you can to promote their ethical, moral, social and financial development?

What do you want to do with your assets? Do you want to

give them to your children, to charity, or will you, by default, give them to the government? If you have put together an estate distribution plan, will your business and other assets be transferred the way you want them to be—whether that transfer is to key employees, children, grandchildren or cousins? And have you carefully considered if that distribution will really be fair?

In making a commitment to the process of effectively transferring your wealth, are you willing to spend the time that is necessary to prepare your children? Are you willing to strike a reasonable balance between the time and energy devoted to business and the time and energy devoted to your family? And are you willing to share your values and skills with your children, and to work toward building a family team?

In seeking the answers to these kinds of questions, I have made reference several times to the functions of a family coach. I've described how a coach can help to smooth family relationships, clarify goals and implement plans. But, for the assistance of a family coach to be most effective, your active participation is essential. You must be willing to look at controversial, emotional or unspoken issues that exist within your family and which have a bearing on their future. Current and potential family conflicts have to be squarely faced and, to the extent possible, reconciled.

If you are willing to do these things, and if you use the tools we provide—forthright communication, family meetings and family partnerships; business apprenticeships for your grown-up children; setting observable and measurable standards for your children's performance; having your children learn to deal with advisers, to name a few—you will begin to develop confidence in this process.

Once you are fully committed, you will gain a great deal of satisfaction as you watch your children's skills and judgment improve in such areas as risk-taking, money management, using advisers and working as a team. As the process continues, you will be more and more confident that your sons and daughters will use your assets responsibly, that they will mature into well-balanced individuals who understand how wealth is acquired and maintained, and the high standards of performance that are necessary to do this. In preparing your children to inherit your wealth, there are many diverse elements to remember. The following Summary of Preparations lists the basic and necessary elements that need to be in place for successful transfer of wealth:

Summary of Preparations

1. My time and energy is balanced between family, business and other interests which bring richness to my life.

2. I hold formal family meetings at least yearly. Any subject is open for discussion at family meetings; money, my net worth and succession issues are examples of discussable topics.

3. The personal values and goals of all family members have been discussed openly within the family; we have agreed upon values we hold in common and we have defined family goals.

4. I have installed a process of training my heirs that will prepare them to manage my wealth. Observable and measurable standards have been established to determine their competence.

5. I have a formal succession plan. A successor has been identified and trained, and the date for my retirement has been set. Family members, my key executives and my advisers are aware of this decision and support it.

6. I have an estate plan which is based upon a family mission. The documents are designed to fullfill this mission and the roles my family and heirs will play in the plan.

7. Family members have discussed and agreed to an inheritance plan that takes into account family bloodlines, in-laws and other beneficiaries, and dilution of ownership.

8. The issue of fair vs. equal inheritance is understood and has been discussed within my family.

9. The issue of control vs. ownership of my business and other assets is understood and has been discussed within my family.

10. I have a will that is current and a process is in place to review and update it annually, in conjunction with our mission.

11. A process is in place with my partners and/or shareholders to review and update all legal agreements annually.

12. All of my adult children participated in the development of my estate and succession plans.

13. My children know and feel comfortable with my trusted advisers and key people.

14. My business Board of Directors includes outsiders for perspective and objectivity, and they know my family well.

15. Five people, in whose business and financial judgment I trust completely, have agreed to advise and assist my family in the event of my death. My family members have met these people and they feel comfortable asking their advice.

16. My business planning includes the successful management of the company during the transition time between my death and my successor's implementation of the succession process.

17. If I died suddenly, my spouse would have no difficulty sustaining her current life style into the foreseeable future.

18. I have run a "fire drill" in regard to my estate and succession planning, and everyone knows what to do and how to respond when I die.

Even after a succession plan and an estate distribution plan are in place, there are some on-going tasks. It's necessary to periodically update goals and plans, and to modify all relevant documents to reflect changes. For example, if a new grandchild arrives, it is easy, amidst all of the excitement, to forget to add that child's name to the will. We recommend that our clients hold family meetings semi-annually or at least annually, including all outside advisers, and review any necessary changes. This review meeting should be formally scheduled and attended by all family members.

With the processes I have described, I am really asking you to take all of the intelligence, energy, creativity and determination that you have so successfully focused on your business and bring it to bear on the challenge of preparing your children and forging a family team.

It has been an extraordinary thing for us at The Williams Group to watch and assist formerly tense, uncooperative, feuding families openly discuss their differences, and then proceed first to tolerance, then mutual respect and, finally, reaffirmation of love for each other. We have watched the most intransigent sons and daughters, and the most stubborn fathers begin to actively help each other. And we've seen individual goals and family goals, for the first time, become complementary rather than antagonistic. Often, this process of forging a family team seems to yield more results in six months than therapy sessions may do in ten years.

As I'm sure you have gathered from this book, we at The Williams Group feel strongly about strengthening the family. The breakdown of family unity is the most prevalent of the problems we encounter. There are many reasons for this, including divorce, parents working in separate places, parents traveling much of the time, children going to school long distances from home—and most importantly, the lack of real communication among family members. Adding to this are the decreasing authority of traditional institutions and the loss of heroes. Family unity has suffered as a result of all of these. This is seen in the increasing number of intra-family legal battles which challenge the emotional as well as the economic survival of the family.

So the family as a unit is breaking down—emotionally, as well as economically. Many years ago, families would sit around the fire and listen to stories. These stories helped to sustain a sense of unity and belonging. Today, our children are involved in worthwhile activities such as athletic teams, dance classes and drama clubs. Parents are also involved in many activities—business, social and charitable—all of which are worthy. But for the most part these are not activities that the family members can participate in together. No one is creating the myths, stories and traditions that create and sustain family unity.

Just as any business needs long-term goals and a mission in order to succeed, so do families need reasons to build a future together. Over the years we have seen parents provide generously for their heirs, but what we have found missing is provision for how the children and grandchildren can act together to further common goals.

One of the tasks of The Williams Group is to encourage the creation of family missions, which respect both individuality and shared purpose. By creating family traditions and missions, family diversity becomes a strength and a joy, and family members share a bond that is strengthened by communication, trust and love. No matter how disfunctional a family initially is, we have never seen the re-emergence of the family, as a unit, fail if all members are committed to this process.

An Example of a Family Mission/Operations Statement

The Purpose of Family Assets

We believe that the purposes of our family assets are to promote the welfare of our immediate family members, of our extended family, of our employees, of our community, of our nation and of all Mankind. To enjoy the benefits of our family assets, all family members will be required to learn the responsible use and management of money to further these goals, and to actively participate in the philanthropic endeavors of the family.

The Importance of Communication

We acknowledge the vital importance of maintaining open and sincere communication among family members. We pledge to respect the opinions of all family members and to provide a continuing forum for these opinions to be expressed. When conflicts occur, we agree to use procedures of conflict resolution in order to arrive at a family consensus.

The Family Team

We understand that the individual goals of family members and the common goals of the family are both legitimate and important. However, we agree that, in general, family goals take precedence over individual goals, and we pledge to work together to build and maintain a close, cohesive family team.

The Family Business

We understand that our primary business goal is to provide

the highest quality of service to our customers, and that in order to do this, we must maintain a thriving, healthy, efficient, profitable company. We agree that all company officers and employees will be required to maintain the highest ethical standards in all business activities. We futher agree that if conflicts should occur between the needs of personal family members and the needs of the company (as defined by its officers), then the company needs shall take precedence.

We acknowledge and respect the contribution of our employees to the success of the company, and we pledge to assume a high level of responsibility for their welfare and the furtherance of their careers. As the company succeeds, we wish them to succeed, and to that end we will maintain a profit-sharing and/or ownership system for this purpose.

Family members will be offered positions in the company only after they have acquired the necessary skills and experience, as defined by observable and measurable standards. Compensation for family members will be strictly determined by company policies and will not be subject to personal influence by family members.

Inheritance and the Family Bloodline

We agree that in-laws will not be excluded from inheritance because they are outside the family bloodline. Bloodline heirs and in-laws will be treated alike in that their rewards and responsibilities will be in proportion to their contribution not only to the company but to the overall family welfare. While we understand the importance of contributions to the company, we also agree that non-business contributions to family welfare are of great importance and will be rewarded accordingly.

Personal Growth

We understand that in order to accomplish our individual and family goals, each of us must be willing to improve our ability to communicate clearly, to handle family responsibilities competently, to treat each other with respect and tolerance, and to help each other in any way we can. And most importantly, we understand that learning to love each other is the basis for real success in all our endeavors, and we pledge to do this to the best of our ability.

Our Reluctance to Ask for Help

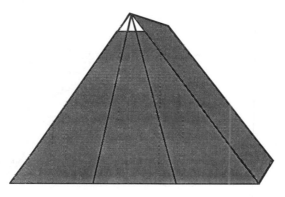

| Preparing Heirs | Trust and Communication | Estate/Succession Planning |

The pyramid—our symbol for the systematic implementation of the Integrated Wealth Transfer Process™—is not yet complete. Before we complete it, there are a few points I have already mentioned, but which warrant a bit of elaboration.

Back in Chapter 5, I mentioned that during thirty-plus years of dealing with families I have only once met an entrepreneur who really felt money was more important than his family—most entrepreneurs care, deeply, about their families. Similarly, most entrepreneurs want to see the wealth they have built up over their lifetimes managed and used wisely, for the benefit of their heirs. Yet many entrepreneurs avoid doing what is necessary to enable these positive results. Why?

Over these years I have had the privilege of meeting large numbers of businessmen, businesswomen and executives who have been very successful in their chosen field. When I have inquired about their families, they have mostly replied positively, like this:

"Why, yes, my two oldest, Michael and Jamie, are doing fine." And, "Anne's as happy as a clam—haven't heard a word of complaint in years."

But when I have had occasion to speak to the other family members, a different picture emerges. Jamie, the eldest, age 29, told me, "No, we don't tell Dad the truth—we can't. Why? Because we don't want to hurt him."

"But Jamie, isn't that going to be a terrible shock to your Dad? He's counting on both of you remaining in the business."

"Yes, it will be—and I feel bad about it. But what can I do?"

His 27-year-old brother, Michael, was more outspoken. "Look, I've been working for the family business for six years and I still have no idea of how profitable we are or even what our sales figures are. Dad has promised to let me in on some of the decision-making, but he hasn't and I know he won't!"

"Why do you think he won't?"

"Dad won't talk about it—he always finds excuses. I suppose I could come right out and challenge him...you know, force him to address these issues, but it's his company...if that's the way he wants it, okay—but I want out."

When I talked to his wife, Anne, she wasn't exactly happy as a clam. "Well, the money is wonderful, but Charlie spends so much time at the office or traveling, I don't even know him anymore. I can't remember the last time we had a weekend together—I mean, just the two of us. I tried hinting in the past, but he doesn't really listen. So I keep up the house, do my charity work and I don't complain. "

When I mentioned to Charlie that things might not be the way he described them, he refused to believe it. "Why I've brought flowers home for Anne every week for...for the last twenty years or so. If she'd been feeling bad about something, I would have known it."

Psychologists call this lack of awareness denial. It's when we consciously or subconsciously ignore and avoid problems rather than face them.

Sometimes we are very aware of issues among family members but we avoid doing anything about them because we're afraid of opening a Pandora's box—all the bad stuff may come pouring out.

But if a family has issues that have been buried and not addressed, they are eventually going to come out, one way or another. If we continue to avoid them, they'll fester and grow, and someday in the future they'll burst out into the open, causing great family strife. Many times this results in the destruction of the family business as well as damaging long-term family relationships. So we have to make a decision: continue avoiding family problems and let the kids deal with them in the future when they burst open; or deal with them now, within the safe environment of professional coaching.

Sometimes family problems are subtle, sometimes only partial. For example, trust and communication among family members may be good, in general, but lacking in one or more specific areas that have, in effect, become taboo. Or, in terms of our wealth transfer pyramid, two sides may be in excellent shape—say, Trust and Communication, and Estate Planning—while the side having to do with Preparing Heirs needs attention.

The point I want to make here is this. Over the years we have worked with families with serious problems as well as many families that are in relatively good shape. But it is a rare family that has got it all covered; almost invariably, some necessary aspects of successful wealth transfer have been neglected.

These neglected areas often prevent the family from being close and from working effectively for shared goals, and they will have a negative influence on the successful transfer of family wealth to children and grandchildren.

We each need to find out what our children, spouses and other family members are really thinking. What are their unvoiced concerns, their needs and their dreams? We each need to look closely at our own situations—and begin to reverse the state of denial.

Denial is not the only reason for inaction; there are many others. I feel they are important, so I'm going to list them in bold type.

- **Denying that family problems exist**
- **Belief that I can handle my family problems without outside help**
- **Belief that I am the only one who can solve my family's**

problems

- Belief that there is no one outside the family who is qualified to help
- Fear that I will look bad if I appear to need help with my family
- Fear that my request for help may be rejected
- Belief that others should know my needs without my having to ask
- Fear of opening a Pandora's box by bringing family problems into the open
- Fear of being in debt to the person or persons who help me
- Fear of family secrets becoming known to others
- Procrastinating
- Unwillingness to spend the time, energy or money that is required to solve family problems
- Belief that it is too early to begin the process
- Resignation — belief that my family's problems are unsolvable

If you share one or more of these for not acting, you are not alone—they are quite common. But I'd like to relate them to something I said in the Introduction to this book. Remember how I was asked, during an exercise for company managers, to try to juggle a bunch of silk scarves? After about three minutes of dropping the scarves on the floor and picking them up, I decided it was a pointless exercise—a waste of time, so I stopped. My instructor asked me if I felt as exasperated as I looked. I told him, yes, that I didn't see the point of my standing there, throwing scarves into the air and picking them up again.

He then asked me if I was a master juggler or even a minimally competent juggler, to which I responded, "no." "In view of that," he said, "shouldn't you expect lots of scarves to be on the floor?" And he suggested that perhaps the cause of my frustration was that I was applying unreasonable standards to myself in assuming I would be competent immediately. The lesson, of course, was that I was not allowing myself to be a beginner, and that if I did so I would be less frustrated, I would learn more quickly and I would be a happier person.

In truth, when it comes to building a cohesive, effective family team, we are all pretty much beginners. And that's okay. To give an analogy, when we hire the services of a master auto mechanic, he may listen to the sound of the engine of our car. It is pinging in a certain way. We both hear it, but it means something different to him than it does to us. He has the experience, the expertise to discern what is happening in the engine from that sound, and we don't. That doesn't make us bad or incompetent persons. It doesn't reflect on our character that we don't understand certain sounds in an auto engine.

The same thing applies to a family coach. Like the master mechanic, the coach is an expert observer. When he sees and hears something during a family interaction, his training allows him to understand what is happening and what action is necessary. When we hear the same thing during a family interaction, it means something quite different to us; we have been in the thick of family matters for many years, and we cannot expect to approach the problem from the same perspective.

Also, unless we, ourselves, have had extensive training and experience in solving family problems, we need to acknowledge that we are beginners. And as beginners, it is not only okay to ask for help—it is the most prudent, effective and efficient action we can take.

Once we are able to acknowledge that we are beginners, the fears and mistaken beliefs that I listed above can be shown to be largely groundless. For example, we don't decide, prior to meeting with the mechanic, if our car engine is fixable or not. We rely on his opinion, and we use that opinion to help us decide what to do. Similarly, we should not presume that family problems are unsolvable until we have heard the opinion of a family coach.

In the beginning of this book I also stated that if you read a cookbook you can try new recipes and reasonably anticipate preparing some satisfying meals without the aid of a chef. Books on legal advice and flying lessons, in contrast, are quick to insist that they are not substitutes for sound, professional assistance. The information I have presented in this book falls into this latter category.

The key to the successful generational transfer of wealth is to place your family within a network of resources that can provide expert assistance that will complement your own commitment to the process.

I will be the first to admit that we don't have all the answers. Some family problems are so deeply-rooted and intractable that they are beyond the scope of our services, or we may fail in some way to communicate the importance of our message. Yet I believe that many of the ideas, stories and procedures I have described in this book will seem relevant to you and your family. I hope you have found the information in this book useful and encouraging, and that you, too, will take up the challenge of preparing your family to manage your wealth. I know that through this process each of you will gain as individuals, and that your family will continue to grow in love and in common purpose.

Roy. O Williams

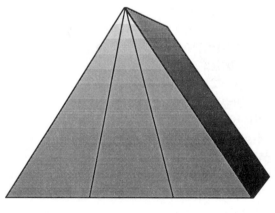

| Preparing | Trust and | Estate/Succession |
| Heirs | Communication | Planning |

Completion of the Integrated Wealth Transfer Process™

Appendix A
Succession Instruments

The Buy/Sell Agreement

The Buy/Sell Agreement is a means for enabling one or more owners of an asset (a company, investment portfolio, property, etc.) to sell their shares to the remaining owners at a future date, in accordance with pre-arranged terms. It is a legal document whose purpose is to allow part owners to sell their interest without destroying the asset and without the need for litigation.

For example, in a partnership, if one partner should die, the surviving partner(s) can agree in advance to buy the business from the heirs of the deceased partner, at a predetermined price. Funding for this buy-out might be needed for several reasons. The business may have to continue paying the deceased partner's salary to his estate and, at the same time, hire and pay another manager to take his place; or there may be an estate tax liability due to the event of a death; or the firm's credit line may be discontinued in the event of a partner's death.

Because the event of a death creates a liability, one of the best ways to provide for it is through life insurance, where that same event also creates a solution.

Regardless of what type of funding vehicle is used, an essential part of a buy/sell agreement is that the funding for a possible future sale is in place.

This agreement involves preparing several projections. For example, what will the value of the business be in the future? This is usually determined by assuming a certain percentage for inflation plus a certain percentage for growth; or, it can be determined by current company value, sales, etc.

The most critical part of the Funded Buy/Sell Agreement is

determining the costs of the funding. Someone must run the actual numbers to come up with a basis for showing a present value cost of alternate funding vehicles

Charitable Foundations

There are basically two kinds of charitable organizations: public charities which either have a broad base of public support or actively support other public charities; and private foundations, which are usually controlled and supported by a single source, such as an individual donor, a family or a company.

Private foundations are further divided into operating foundations and nonoperating foundations. Private nonoperating foundations basically give money to other charitable organizations. In contrast, private operating foundations support programs and activities operated by the foundations themselves. Accordingly, a private operating foundation is able to support virtually any type of charitable activity in which it is actively involved and as long as it is consistent with the foundation's purpose. This type of foundation may also carry over excess income into future years for foundation activities.

A private operating foundation requires more extensive planning in its structure and activities in order to obtain approval from the IRS as a tax exempt organization, but the results are worth the effort. Most charitable foundations in the United States are nonoperating foundations, not because of the difficulties involved with the IRS approval, but simply because many lawyers and tax accountants are unaware of operating foundations. Unless specifically qualified as operating foundations, all private foundations are nonoperating foundations by default.

Creating a charitable foundation satisfies several needs at the same time. First of all, it may avoid the payment of estate taxes upon the death of the father or mother or both (depending on how the estate is set up) by removing assets from the estate prior to death, with a corresponding charitable deduction. When the foundation is set up while dad and mom are still alive, they can get personal satisfaction and recognition from becoming involved with a university, hospital, etc., and at the same time, obtain some current income tax deductions. In addition, by involving their children with the foundation, parents can enable them to gain operating experience and monitor their performance. Finally, if an operating foundation is established, the family can engage in charitable activities created and managed by the foundation and family members can continue operations after the death of the parents.

If, for example, in compliance with IRS rules you transfer five hundred thousand dollars of assets (the actual number isn't important) to a qualifying foundation, any amount given to such a foundation will not be taxable at your death and gift taxes can be avoided as well, even on property with capital gains, with proper planning and observance of the tax rules.

As members of the board, the adult children will help determine how the money is distributed. If the foundation is a nonoperating foundation, they will have to make sure that the foundation gives away all of its income every year.

By participating in the operation of a foundation, adult children learn not just how to give away money, but how to do it responsibly. In addition to giving away money, they are also giving of their time and energy. For the adult children, it is a hands-on course in money-management and assessing and doing something about social needs. If an operating foundation is created, the adult children can also gain firsthand knowledge of charitable and management activity through creating and supervising foundation programs.

The Will Summary

Because of their extensive legalese, wills are usually not readily understood by the layperson who wants a quick read. Many find it hard to remember the precise stipulations of a will years after it has been drawn up For these reasons, I recommend that my clients have their lawyer prepare a one-page, informal summary of the will that is not a legal part of it, but which is simply folded inside of the will and which accompanies it. This summary of the will should state, in simple language, an outline of the client's goals and what the will accomplishes. The purpose of the will summary is to help a client remember what he or she was trying to accomplish with a particular will. If a client's goals have changed since the will was drawn up, and the will needs updating, the summary makes this clear. The need to change a will because of additional children, grandchildren and in-laws, or changes in a client's values, can be identified and the client's lawyer contacted for an update, codicil or new will. The will summary should be updated each time the will is changed.

Appendix B
Recommended
Additional Reading

Beyond Survival, Leon Danco, University Press, Cleveland, 1975

Chicken Soup for the Soul, Vol. I and II, Jack Canfield & Mark Victor Hansen, Health Communications, Inc., Deerfield Beach, FL, 1993

Chop Wood, Carry Water, Rick Fields, Peggy Taylor, Rex Weyler & Rick Ingrasci, St. Martin's Press, New York, *1984*

Creating Effective Boards, John S. Ward, Jossey-Bass, Inc., San Francisco, 1991

Family Foundations at Work, Kelin E. Gersick, John A. Davis & Kevin Seymour, a research report of the California School of Professional Psychology, Whitman Institute, San Francisco, 1990

"Fathers—Not Managers—Know Best," Sue Shellenbarger, Wall Street Journal, September 12, 1991

Flow—The Psychology of Optimum Experience, Mihaly Csikszentmihalyi, Harper Perennials, New York, 1990

Ghandi, The Man, Eknath Easwaran, Nilgiri Press, Petaluma, CA 1978

(The) Golden Ghetto, the Psychology of Affluence, Jessie H. O'Neill, Hazelden, Center City, MN, 1997

Half Time, Bob Buford, Zon Dervan Publishing, Grand Rapids, MI, 1994

Language of Love, Gary Smalley & John Trent, Focus on the Family Publishing, Pomona, CA, 1988

Love and Profit, James A. Autry, Morrow, New York, 1991

Love & Survival, Dean Ornish, M.D., Harper Collins, New York, 1998

Man's Search for Meaning, Victor Frankel, Washington Square Press, New York, 1965

March of Folly, Barbara W. Tuchman, Ballantine Press, New York, 1985

Mastering Change, Ichak Adizes, Adizes Inst. Publications, Santa Monica, CA, 1991

(The) Only Guide to a Winning Investment Strategy You'll Ever Need, Larry E. Swedroe, Truman Talley Books/Dutton, New York, 1998

Sanity, Insanity and Common Sense, Rick Suarez, Roger Mill & Darlene Stewart, Fawcett Columbine, New York, 1987

Servant Leadership, Robert K. Greenleaf, Paulist Press, Ramsey, NJ, 1977

Streams in the Desert Sampler, Mrs. Charles E. Conman, Daybreak Books, Grand Rapids, MI, 1983

Teaching Your Children Responsibility, Teaching Your Children Values, Teaching Your Children Joy, Linda & Richard Eyre, Simon & Shuster, New York, 1994

Unconditional Love, John Powell, Tabor Publishing, Allen, TX, 1978

What Really Matters At Home, Jon & Susan Yates, Weed Publishing, Dallas, 1992

3 Steps to a Strong Family, Linda & Richard Eyre, Simon & Shuster, New York, 1996

Here's how to order additional copies of

For Love & Money: A Comprehensive Guide to the Successful Generational Transfer of Wealth

by Roy O. Williams

Credit card telephone orders (toll free 24-hour service): 888-467-5310
Credit card fax orders (24 hours): (209) 951-9232
Postal orders, please send check or credit card information to:

Bookminders
3620-D West Hammer Lane
Stockton, CA 95219

$29.95 per copy + $4.00 shipping for first copy; $3.00 shipping for each additional copy to same address. Books are shipped by Priority mail. California orders: please add $2.32 sales tax per book for all orders shipped to California addresses.

☐ Master Card   ☐ Visa

Credit card No._____ Exp. Date_____

Your signature _____

Your Name (please print) _____

Address to send book(s)_____

_____

_____

No. of copies ordered _____ If check, am't enclosed _____

Please make checks payable to Bookminders

☐ Please send information on the services of The Williams Group

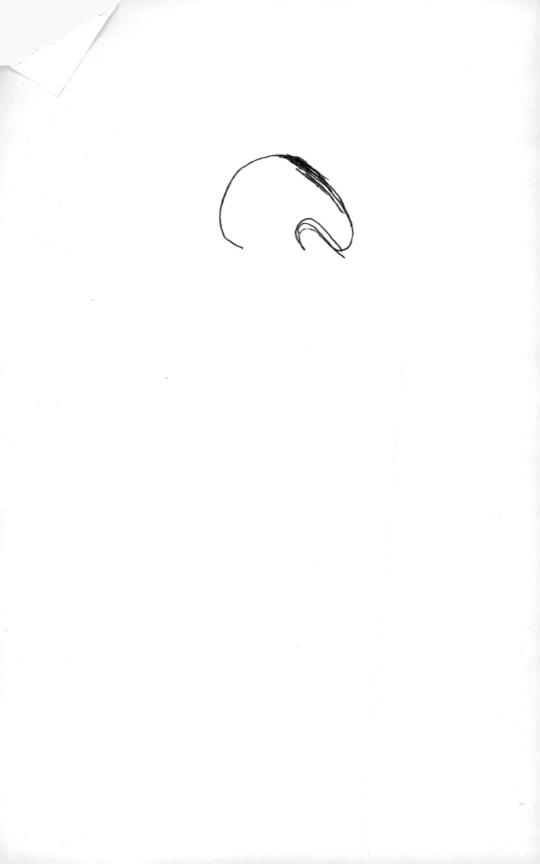